On Course: Targeting Your Success

Professionalism and Human Performance EX-PY 201

Central Christian College of Kansas

Skip Downing

Australia • Brazil • Japan • Korea • Mexico • Singapore • Spain • United Kingdom • United States

On Course: Targeting Your Success: Professionalism and Human Performance EX-PY 201, Central Christian College of Kansas

Skip Downing

Senior Manager, Student Engagement:
Linda deStefano

Manager, Student Engagement:
Julie Dierig

Marketing Manager:
Rachael Kloos

Manager, Premedia:
Kim Fry

Manager, Intellectual Property Project Manager:
Brian Methe

Senior Manager, Production:
Donna M. Brown

Manager, Production:
Terri Daley

On Course: Strategies for Creating Success in College and in Life, 7th Edition
Skip Downing

© 2014 Cengage Learning. All rights reserved.

ALL RIGHTS RESERVED. No part of this work covered by the copyright herein may be reproduced, transmitted, stored or used in any form or by any means graphic, electronic, or mechanical, including but not limited to photocopying, recording, scanning, digitizing, taping, Web distribution, information networks, or information storage and retrieval systems, except as permitted under Section 107 or 108 of the 1976 United States Copyright Act, without the prior written permission of the publisher.

> For product information and technology assistance, contact us at
> **Cengage Learning Customer & Sales Support, 1-800-354-9706**
> For permission to use material from this text or product,
> submit all requests online at **cengage.com/permissions**
> Further permissions questions can be emailed to
> **permissionrequest@cengage.com**

This book contains select works from existing Cengage Learning resources and was produced by Cengage Learning Custom Solutions for collegiate use. As such, those adopting and/or contributing to this work are responsible for editorial content accuracy, continuity and completeness.

Compilation © 2014 Cengage Learning
ISBN: 978-1-305-29949-8

WCN: 01-100-101

Cengage Learning
20 Channel Center Street
Boston, MA 02210
USA

Cengage Learning is a leading provider of customized learning solutions with office locations around the globe, including Singapore, the United Kingdom, Australia, Mexico, Brazil, and Japan. Locate your local office at:
international.cengage.com/region.

Cengage Learning products are represented in Canada by Nelson Education, Ltd.
For your lifelong learning solutions, visit **www.cengage.com/custom**.
Visit our corporate website at **www.cengage.com**.

Brief Contents

Chapter 1 Getting On Course to Your Success 1
Chapter 2 Accepting Personal Responsibility 23
Chapter 3 Discovering Self-Motivation.. 34
Chapter 5 Employing Interdependence... 54
Chapter 6 Gaining Self-Awareness 63
Chapter 7 Adopting Lifelong Learning 81
Chapter 9 Staying On Course to Your Success... 96

Taking the First Step

Focus Questions What does "success" mean to you? When you achieve your greatest success, what will you have, what will you be doing, and what kind of person will you be?

Congratulations on choosing to attend college! With this choice, you've begun a journey that can lead to great personal and professional success.

WHAT IS SUCCESS?

I've asked many college graduates, "What did success mean to you when you were an undergraduate?" Here are some typical answers:

When I was in college, success to me was . . .

. . . getting all A's and B's.
. . . making two free-throws to win the conference basketball tournament.
. . . having a great social life.
. . . parenting two great kids and still making the dean's list.
. . . being the first person in my family to earn a college degree.

Notice that each response emphasizes *outer success*: high grades, sports victories, popularity, and college degrees. These successes are public, visible achievements that allow the world to judge one's abilities and worth.

I've also asked college graduates, "If you could repeat your college years, what would you do differently?" Here are some typical answers:

If I had a chance to do college over, I would . . .

. . . focus on learning instead of just getting good grades.
. . . major in engineering, the career I had a passion for.
. . . constantly ask myself how I could use what I was learning to enhance my life and the lives of the people I love.
. . . discover my personal values.
. . . learn more about the world I live in and more about myself . . . especially more about myself!

> College is a place where a student ought to learn not so much how to make a living, but how to live.
>
> *Dr. William A. Nolen*

Notice that the focus some years after graduation often centers on *inner success*: enjoying learning, following personal interests, focusing on personal values, and creating more fulfilling lives. These successes are private, invisible victories that offer a deep sense of personal contentment.

Only with hindsight do most college graduates realize that, to be completely satisfying, success must occur both in the visible world and in the invisible spaces within our minds and hearts. This book, then, is about how to achieve both outer and inner success in college and in life.

To that end, I suggest the following simple definition of success: **Success is staying on course to your desired outcomes and experiences.** Maybe you'd like to earn a college degree or start your own business or marry and have six kids. Maybe you'd like to experience joy or confidence or love. Maybe you'd like to be seen by others as a "self-made" person who achieved success by your efforts alone. Maybe you'd prefer to experience being a valued member of a group that is loyal and committed to one another. Regardless of what your desired outcomes and experiences may be, following the time-tested strategies presented in *On Course* will help you achieve them.

As a college instructor, I have seen thousands of students arrive on campus with dreams, then struggle, fail, and fade away. I've seen thousands more come to college with dreams, pass their courses, and graduate, having done little more than cram their brains with information that's promptly forgotten after the final exam. They've earned degrees, but in more important ways they have remained unchanged.

Our primary responsibility in life, I suggest, is to realize the incredible potential with which each of us is born. All of our experiences, especially those during college, can contribute to the creation of our best selves.

On Course shows how to use your college experience as a laboratory experiment. In this laboratory you'll learn and apply proven strategies that help you create success—academically, personally, and professionally. I'm not saying it'll be easy, but you're about to learn strategies that have made a difference in the lives of thousands of students before you. So get ready to change the outcomes of your life and the quality of your experiences along the way! Get ready to create success as *you* define it.

To begin, consider a curious puzzle: Two students enter a college class on the first day of the semester. Both appear to have similar intelligence, backgrounds, and abilities. The weeks slide by, and the semester ends. Surprisingly, one student soars and the other sinks. One fulfills his potential; the other falls short. Why do students with similar aptitudes perform so differently? More important, which of these students is you?

Teachers observe this puzzle in every class. I bet you've seen it, too, not only in school, but wherever people gather. Some people have a knack for achievement. Others wander about confused and disappointed, unable to create the success they claim they want. Clearly, having potential does not guarantee success.

What, then, are the essential ingredients of success?

THE POWER OF CHOICE

The main ingredient in all success is wise choices. That's because the quality of our lives is determined by the quality of the choices we make on a daily basis. Successful people stay on course to their destinations by wisely choosing their beliefs and behaviors.

Do beliefs cause behaviors, or do behaviors lead to beliefs? Like the chicken and the egg, it's hard to say which came first. This much is clear: Once you choose a positive belief or an effective behavior, you usually find yourself in a cycle of success. Positive beliefs lead to effective behaviors. Effective behaviors lead to success. And success reinforces the positive beliefs.

> There is only one success—to be able to spend your life in your own way.
>
> *Christopher Morely*

> The deepest personal defeat suffered by human beings is constituted by the difference between what one was capable of becoming and what one has in fact become.
>
> *Ashley Montagu*

Here's an example showing how the choice of beliefs and behaviors determines results. Until 1954, most track-and-field experts believed it was impossible for a person to run a mile in less than four minutes. On May 6, 1954, however, Roger Bannister of England ran a mile in the world-record time of 3:59.4. Once Bannister had proven that running a four-minute mile was possible, within months, many other runners also broke the four-minute barrier. In other words, once runners chose a new belief (a person *can* run a mile in less than four minutes), they pushed their physical abilities, and suddenly the impossible became possible. By the way, the present world's record, set in 1999 by Hicham El Guerrouj of Morocco, is an amazing 3:43.13. So much for limiting beliefs!

Consider another example. After a disappointing test score, a struggling student thinks, "I knew I couldn't do college math!" This belief will likely cause the student to miss classes and neglect assignments. These self-defeating behaviors will lead to even lower test scores, reinforcing the negative beliefs. This student, caught in a cycle of failure, is now in grave danger of failing math.

In that same class, however, someone with no better math ability is passing the course because this student believes she *can* pass college math. Consequently, she chooses positive behaviors such as attending every class, completing all of her assignments, getting a tutor, and asking the instructor for help. Her grades go up, confirming her empowering belief. The cycle of success has this student on course to passing math.

Someone once said, "If you keep doing what you've been doing, you'll keep getting what you've been getting." That's why if you want to improve your life (and why else would you attend college?), you may need to change some of your beliefs and behaviors. Conscious experimentation will teach you which ones are already working well for you and which ones need revision. Once these new beliefs and behaviors become a habit, you'll find yourself in the cycle of success, on course to creating your dreams in college and in life.

> Life is a self-fulfilling prophesy... in the long run you usually get what you expect.
>
> Denis Waitley

WRITE A GREAT LIFE

College offers the perfect opportunity to design a life worth living. A time-tested tool for this purpose is a journal, a written record of your thoughts and feelings, hopes and dreams. Journal writing is a way to explore your life in depth and discover your best "self." This self-awareness will enable you to make wise choices about what to keep doing and what to change.

Many people who keep journals do what is called "free writing." They simply write whatever thoughts come to mind. This approach can be extremely valuable for exploring issues present in one's mind at any given moment.

In *On Course*, however, you will write a guided journal. This approach is like going on a journey with an experienced guide. Your guide takes you places and shows you sights you might never have discovered on your own.

Before writing each journal entry, you'll read an article about proven success strategies. Then you'll apply the strategies to your own life by completing the guided journal entry that follows the article. Here are five guidelines for creating a meaningful journal:

- **Copy the directions for each step into your journal (just the bold print):** When you find your journal in a drawer or computer file 20 years from now, having the directions in your journal will help you make sense of what you've written. Underline or bold the directions to distinguish them from your answers.
- **Be spontaneous:** Write whatever comes to mind in response to the directions. Imagine pouring liquid thoughts into your journal without pausing to edit or rewrite. Unlike public writings, such as an English composition or a history research paper, your journal is a private document written primarily for your own benefit.
- **Be honest:** As you write, tell yourself the absolute truth; honesty leads to your most significant discoveries about yourself and your success.
- **Be creative:** Add favorite quotations, sayings, and poems. Use color, drawings, clip art, and photographs. Express your best creative "self."
- **Dive deep:** When you think you have exhausted a topic, write more. Your most valuable thoughts will often take the longest to surface. So, most of all—DIVE DEEP!

> Journal work is an excellent approach to uncovering hidden truths about ourselves.
>
> *Marsha Sinetar*

For easy reference, these five important guidelines are also printed on the inside back cover of this book.

Whether you handwrite your journal or compose it on a computer, I urge you to keep all of your journal entries together in one book or file. If you do, one day many years from now, you'll have the extraordinary pleasure of reading this autobiography of your growing wisdom about creating success in college and in life.

ASSESS YOURSELF

Before we examine the choices of successful students, take a few minutes to complete the self-assessment questionnaire on the next two pages. Your scores will identify behaviors and beliefs that support your success. They'll also point out behaviors and beliefs you may want to change to achieve more of your potential in college and in life. In the last chapter, you will have an opportunity to repeat this self-assessment and compare your two scores. I think you're going to be pleasantly surprised!

This self-assessment is not a test. There are no right or wrong answers. The questions simply give you an opportunity to create an accurate and current self-portrait. Be absolutely honest and have fun with this activity, for it is the first step on an exciting journey to a richer, more personally fulfilling life.

SELF-ASSESSMENT

Visit www.cengagebrain.com to access this self-assessment online through CourseMate for *On Course*.

Read the following statements and score each one according to how true or false you believe it is about you. To get an accurate picture of yourself, consider what IS true about you (not what you want to be true). Remember, there are no right or wrong answers. Assign each statement a number from 0 to 10, as follows:

Totally False ← 0 1 2 3 4 5 6 7 8 9 10 → **Totally True**

1. _____ I control how successful I will be.
2. _____ I'm not sure why I'm in college.
3. _____ I spend most of my time doing important things.
4. _____ When I encounter a challenging problem, I try to solve it by myself.
5. _____ When I get off course from my goals and dreams, I realize it right away.
6. _____ I'm not sure how I prefer to learn.
7. _____ Whether I'm happy or not depends mostly on me.
8. _____ I'll truly accept myself only after I eliminate my faults and weaknesses.
9. _____ Forces out of my control (such as poor teaching) are the cause of low grades I receive in school.
10. _____ I place great value on getting my college degree.
11. _____ I don't need to write things down because I can remember what I need to do.
12. _____ I have a network of people in my life that I can count on for help.
13. _____ If I have habits that hinder my success, I'm not sure what they are.
14. _____ When I don't like the way an instructor teaches, I know how to learn the subject anyway.
15. _____ When I get very angry, sad, or afraid, I do or say things that create a problem for me.
16. _____ When I think about performing an upcoming challenge (such as taking a test), I usually see myself doing well.
17. _____ When I have a problem, I take positive actions to find a solution.
18. _____ I don't know how to set effective short-term and long-term goals.
19. _____ I am organized.
20. _____ When I take a difficult course in school, I study alone.
21. _____ I'm aware of beliefs I have that hinder my success.
22. _____ I'm not sure how to think critically and analytically about complex topics.
23. _____ When choosing between doing an important school assignment or something really fun, I do the school assignment.
24. _____ I break promises that I make to myself or to others.
25. _____ I make poor choices that keep me from getting what I really want in life.
26. _____ I expect to do well in my college classes.
27. _____ I lack self-discipline.
28. _____ I listen carefully when other people are talking.
29. _____ I'm stuck with any habits of mine that hinder my success.
30. _____ My intelligence is something about myself that I can improve.

31. _____ I often feel bored, anxious, or depressed.
32. _____ I feel just as worthwhile as any other person.
33. _____ Forces outside of me (such as luck or other people) control how successful I will be.
34. _____ College is an important step on the way to accomplishing my goals and dreams.
35. _____ I spend most of my time doing unimportant things.
36. _____ I am aware of how to show respect to people who are different from me (race, religion, sexual orientation, age, etc.).
37. _____ I can be off course from my goals and dreams for quite a while without realizing it.
38. _____ I know how I prefer to learn.
39. _____ My happiness depends mostly on what's happened to me lately.
40. _____ I accept myself just as I am, even with my faults and weaknesses.
41. _____ I am the cause of low grades I receive in school.
42. _____ If I lose my motivation in college, I don't know how I'll get it back.
43. _____ I have a written self-management system that helps me get important things done on time.
44. _____ I seldom interact with people who are different from me.
45. _____ I'm aware of the habits I have that hinder my success.
46. _____ If I don't like the way an instructor teaches, I'll probably do poorly in the course.
47. _____ When I'm very angry, sad, or afraid, I know how to manage my emotions so I don't do anything I'll regret later.
48. _____ When I think about performing an upcoming challenge (such as taking a test), I usually see myself doing poorly.
49. _____ When I have a problem, I complain, blame others, or make excuses.
50. _____ I know how to set effective short-term and long-term goals.
51. _____ I am disorganized.
52. _____ When I take a difficult course in school, I find a study partner or join a study group.
53. _____ I'm unaware of beliefs I have that hinder my success.
54. _____ I know how to think critically and analytically about complex topics.
55. _____ I often feel happy and fully alive.
56. _____ I keep promises that I make to myself or to others.
57. _____ When I have an important choice to make, I use a decision-making process that analyzes possible options and their likely outcomes.
58. _____ I don't expect to do well in my college classes.
59. _____ I am a self-disciplined person.
60. _____ I get distracted easily when other people are talking.
61. _____ I know how to change habits of mine that hinder my success.
62. _____ Everyone is born with a certain amount of intelligence, and there's not really much you can do to change that.
63. _____ When choosing between doing an important school assignment or something really fun, I usually do something fun.
64. _____ I feel less worthy than other people.

Transfer your scores to the scoring sheets on the next page. For each of the eight areas, total your scores in columns A and B. Then total your final scores as shown in the sample on the next page.

SELF-ASSESSMENT SCORING SHEET

SAMPLE

A	B
6. _8_	29. _3_
14. _5_	35. _3_
21. _6_	50. _6_
73. _9_	56. _2_

_28_ + 40 − _14_ = 54

SCORE #1: ACCEPTING PERSONAL RESPONSIBILITY

A	B
1. ___	9. ___
17. ___	25. ___
41. ___	33. ___
57. ___	49. ___

___ + 40 − ___ = ___

SCORE #2: DISCOVERING SELF-MOTIVATION

A	B
10. ___	2. ___
26. ___	18. ___
34. ___	42. ___
50. ___	58. ___

___ + 40 − ___ = ___

SCORE #3: MASTERING SELF-MANAGEMENT

A	B
3. ___	11. ___
19. ___	27. ___
43. ___	35. ___
59. ___	51. ___

___ + 40 − ___ = ___

SCORE #4: EMPLOYING INTERDEPENDENCE

A	B
12. ___	4. ___
28. ___	20. ___
36. ___	44. ___
52. ___	60. ___

___ + 40 − ___ = ___

SCORE #5: GAINING SELF-AWARENESS

A	B
5. ___	13. ___
21. ___	29. ___
45. ___	37. ___
61. ___	53. ___

___ + 40 − ___ = ___

SCORE #6: ADOPTING LIFELONG LEARNING

A	B
14. ___	6. ___
30. ___	22. ___
38. ___	46. ___
54. ___	62. ___

___ + 40 − ___ = ___

SCORE #7: DEVELOPING EMOTIONAL INTELLIGENCE

A	B
7. ___	15. ___
23. ___	31. ___
47. ___	39. ___
55. ___	63. ___

___ + 40 − ___ = ___

SCORE #8: BELIEVING IN MYSELF

A	B
16. ___	8. ___
32. ___	24. ___
40. ___	48. ___
56. ___	64. ___

___ + 40 − ___ = ___

INTERPRETING YOUR SCORES

A score of . . .

- **0–39** Indicates an area where your choices will **seldom** keep you on course.
- **40–63** Indicates an area where your choices will **sometimes** keep you on course.
- **64–80** Indicates an area where your choices will **usually** keep you on course.

CHOICES OF SUCCESSFUL STUDENTS

SUCCESSFUL STUDENTS...	STRUGGLING STUDENTS...
accept personal responsibility, seeing themselves as the primary cause of their outcomes and experiences.	see themselves as victims, believing that what happens to them is determined primarily by external forces such as fate, luck, and powerful others.
discover self-motivation, finding purpose in their lives by discovering personally meaningful goals and dreams.	have difficulty sustaining motivation, often feeling depressed, frustrated, and/or resentful about a lack of direction in their lives.
master self-management, consistently planning and taking purposeful actions in pursuit of their goals and dreams.	seldom identify specific actions needed to accomplish a desired outcome, and when they do, they tend to procrastinate.
employ interdependence, building mutually supportive relationships that help them achieve their goals and dreams (while helping others do the same).	are solitary, seldom requesting, even rejecting, offers of assistance from those who could help.
gain self-awareness, consciously employing behaviors, beliefs, and attitudes that keep them on course.	make important choices unconsciously, being directed by self-sabotaging habits and outdated life scripts.
adopt lifelong learning, finding valuable lessons and wisdom in nearly every experience they have.	resist learning new ideas and skills, viewing learning as fearful or boring rather than as mental play.
develop emotional intelligence, effectively managing their emotions in support of their goals and dreams.	live at the mercy of strong emotions, such as anger, depression, anxiety, or a need for instant gratification.
believe in themselves, seeing themselves as capable, lovable, and unconditionally worthy human beings.	doubt their competence and personal value, feeling inadequate to create their desired outcomes and experiences.

CULTURE SHOCK

What happens, then, when *they* don't do things the way *we* do? Or, what happens when *we* don't do things the way *they* do? In other words, what happens when different cultures clash?

Here's an example of surface cultures clashing: You're traveling with a group of American students in China. In the province of Guangdong, students from a local university invite your group to join them for a meal. You've saved your appetite for a grand feast, and after many tasty appetizers, your hosts proudly present the main dish. *What the heck is that? Oh my god . . . they're serving a barbequed dog!* Chances are, you've just experienced a clash of surface cultures. Your mind races with judgments about what is appropriate, right, or good to serve for dinner. In North American culture, dogs are pets. We all know the unwritten rule: People don't eat their pets (let alone serve them to guests).

Now, consider a clash of deep cultures. At your college, you join a math study group that includes Tariq, a young man from Saudi Arabia. You're explaining how you solved homework problem number three when Tariq excitedly interrupts: "What you are saying can also work for numbers four and five!" Tariq takes over the conversation, and you wait quietly until he finishes. Then you've barely begun explaining your approach to problem six when Tariq, with great enthusiasm, cuts you off again. A few minutes later, he butts in once more, and now you're steaming. You've just experienced a clash of deep cultures: judgments about what is appropriate, right, or good to do in a conversation. The unwritten rule in some cultures (e.g., United States, English-speaking Canada, and England) is that speakers take turns speaking. In other cultures (e.g., Middle East, Southern France, and Spain), interruptions are expected. In fact, if someone doesn't interrupt, others may assume the person doesn't care about the subject under discussion.

Culture shock is the upset and stress we experience when confronted with behaviors and beliefs that differ significantly from our own. Because we are quite sure that our way is right, a typical response to culture shock is judgment: Tariq is self-centered, inconsiderate, and rude. As judgments fly and our discomfort increases, typical responses are fight (*I'm not putting up with this!*) or flight (*I'm outta here!*) Seldom is either choice helpful in achieving our desired outcomes and experiences.

Which brings us to the importance of understanding the culture and traditions of higher education in North America.

THE CULTURE OF HIGHER EDUCATION

Because college is a unique culture, expect some challenges as you adapt. Most differences in surface culture will be pretty obvious. For example, like all cultures, higher education has its own language, so you'll probably hear words that

---

Culture shock can take its toll on us. It can make us feel anxious, disoriented, and depressed. . . . Minimizing culture shock requires new knowledge and insights as well as a certain degree of flexibility.

Richard Bucher,
Building Cultural Intelligence

sound foreign to you. Suppose an instructor tells your class, "The directions for your first paper are posted on Moodle. Be sure to do it in MLA format." These directions make little sense if you don't know the lingo. But it's not really that complicated. Here's what those familiar with college culture know:

Moodle is a computer software program that allows colleges to offer class content on the Internet. (A similar program is called BlackBoard.) If your instructor doesn't provide directions for accessing course information posted on the Internet, contact the folks in your campus computer lab for help.

MLA format is a set of guidelines provided by the Modern Language Association (MLA) for how writers in the humanities should identify research sources. By the way, writers in the sciences use a different format, one provided by the APA (American Psychological Association). For more information about these formats, you can ask a librarian or do an Internet search for help.

To learn additional surface features of college culture, see "Wise Choices in College: College Customs" (pages 34–38). Following the suggestions there will help you avoid a number of bumps and potholes in your journey through higher education.

Now for a few words about deep culture. As suggested earlier, these differences will be less obvious. In fact, you may find yourself off course and not even realize that the cause is a clash of deep cultures. That's why the sooner you learn the culture of higher education in general, and the culture of your college in particular, the better you'll be able to make wise choices and stay on course to academic success.

Throughout *On Course* we will be exploring the deep culture of higher education in North America, but let's take a look at one example here. Keep in mind that statements about any culture are generalizations. As with all generalizations, they will likely vary for individual campuses and certainly vary for individual instructors. However, you can use the following example (and those presented throughout the book) to gage where your college—or an instructor—stands in regard to each of these mindsets and make your choices accordingly.

One element of deep college culture that's almost sure to be important at your college is a high regard for intellectual curiosity. I've asked literally thousands of educators, "What inner qualities would you like your students to have?" *Intellectual curiosity* is a near unanimous choice. Your instructors want you to be as curious about their subject as they are. Or at least curious about something. They want you to think deeply about life. They want you to ask thoughtful questions and pursue the answers with enthusiasm. Questions like *Why? How do you know? Who else believes this? What's the cause? What's another explanation? When might this not be so? How can I use this?* Bottom line: Intellectual curiosity is greatly prized in the deep culture of higher education.

Toto, I have a feeling we're not in Kansas anymore.

Dorothy, in The Wizard of Oz

Schools, like ethnic groups, have their own cultures: languages, ways of doing things, values, attitudes toward time, standards of appropriate behavior, and so on. As participants in schools, students are expected to adopt, share, and exhibit these cultural patterns. If they do not or cannot, they are likely to be censured and made to feel uncomfortable in a variety of ways.

Jean Moule, Cultural Competence

A Dozen Differences Between High School and College Culture	
High School Culture—Assumes Immaturity	College Culture—Assumes Maturity
Students attend high school because they are required to by their parents or by law.	Students usually attend college because of a personal choice.
Teachers offer students many reminders to complete assignments.	Instructors give assignments and expect students to hand them in on time without reminders.
Teachers spend time disciplining students who create disruptions.	Instructors do not tolerate disruptive students and may bar them from the class.
Students typically spend 30 or more hours in class each week, and teachers cover the majority of course content during class.	Students typically spend 15 or fewer hours in class each week, and instructors expect students to learn the majority of course content outside of class.
Teachers and parents manage much of the students' time.	Students manage their own time.
Teachers are often pressured to "teach to the test" so that students can pass standardized assessments.	Instructors have more "academic freedom" in what and how they teach.
Academic standards are not always high, and savvy students often get good grades with little effort.	Academic standards are usually high, and all students need to figure out how to meet these challenging standards.
Family and friends provide students with advice or solutions for academic, social, and other problems.	Students solve their own problems or seek help at one of many support services provided by the college.
Students' choice of courses is relatively limited by graduation requirements.	Students have greater freedom to choose the courses they take and drop those they don't want to complete.
Teachers and parents minimize distractions that might otherwise hinder students' success.	Students must deal with distractions on their own, including parties, television, video games, Internet surfing, dating, sports, Facebook, drinking, road trips, and hanging out.
Educational costs are paid for by taxpayers, including text books.	Educational costs, including text books, are paid for by the student, the student's family, and/or by financial aid for which the student applies and, in some cases, must pay back.
Students have few choices.	Students have many choices.

So, how might a student clash with this aspect of deep college culture? Here's just one possibility. A student gets back a writing assignment, and the grade is lower than he expected. A *lot* lower. *Darn,* he thinks, *I spent hours writing that paper. What does the instructor expect anyway? This would have been at least a B in high school. Probably an A! What is she thinking!* For an answer, let's visit the instructor at home the night before where we catch her reading that very student's paper: *Darn, she thinks, this essay is so boring. It's as though the writer simply copied sentences from various Internet sites and strung them together as an essay. His main concern seems to be having enough words to fulfill the assignment. Where's the writer's curiosity, his passion, his quest for answers? What is he thinking!*

The student is discouraged, and the instructor is too. They both have good intentions yet neither may realize the problem: deep cultures clashing. He wants to get a good grade. She wants to see intellectual curiosity.

CHOICES AND CULTURE

The choices recommended in *On Course* exist as possibilities for every human being. However, here's a heads up: Sometimes an option presented in these pages may clash with your own cultural or individual programming. As such, you may judge them as inappropriate, wrong, or bad. For example, in Chapter 5 you'll read about the benefits of interdependence. This principle suggests that creating mutually supportive relationships can enhance your chances for success. However, if you've been raised in traditional North American culture, your default choice is likely to be independence. In fact, asking for help may feel so uncomfortable that pursuing your success alone may seem to be your only choice. There is certainly a time for *in*dependence, but what if choosing *inter*-dependence at the right time can improve your chances for success?

> If all you have is a hammer, everything looks like a nail.
>
> *Carl Jung*

Here's another example. As you've learned, *On Course* presents success principles and practices. Then it asks you to reflect on these strategies by writing guided journal entries. If you've been raised in a working-class culture, and especially if you are young and male, your programming probably favors action over reflection. Thus, writing reflective journals may feel uncomfortable. There is certainly a time for action, but what if choosing reflection at the right time can improve your chances for success?

Here's the point: Empowered people appreciate having choices . . . as many as possible. Having options usually increases anyone's likelihood for success, especially when seeking success in a new culture. At each fork in the road, empowered people decide which choice—from among many—will most likely help them create the outcomes and experiences they want.

In this course you will learn much about the surface- and deep-culture rules of higher education. In the process, you'll come to understand what natives of this unique culture judge to be appropriate, right, and good (and, conversely, what they believe is inappropriate, wrong, and bad). At some point early in the process, you may feel that you don't belong in this culture . . . you might even feel unwelcome. Just know that this is a natural part of figuring out and fitting into any new culture. If your culture is very different from the culture of higher education, at some point you may even ask yourself, "How much of my culture do I need to give up in order to succeed in college?"

It's up to each of us to decide when to follow a choice of our culture, when to follow a choice of another culture, or when to honor a choice born of our own wisdom. Whatever their source, the more options you have to choose from, the more empowered you will be to create the life you want.

> Life is the sum of all your choices.
>
> *Albert Camus*

Journal Entry 2

In this activity you will explore various aspects of surface and deep culture that you have experienced in school.

1. Contrast the surface culture of the last school you attended with that of your present school. From the following list, choose two or more surface-level features that are different for the two schools. Then, in a separate paragraph for each feature, explain how the two schools are different.

Number of students in a class	Age of students
Race or ethnicity of students	Economic class of students
Courses offered	Amount of homework
Popular out-of-school activities	Teachers' treatment of students
Alcohol	Academic preparation of educators
In-groups	Religions
Clothes	Food
Languages spoken	Dialects spoken
Sports	Amount of writing assigned
Amount of reading assigned	Drugs
Architecture of buildings	Favorite music
Holidays observed	Out-groups
Attendance policy	Methods of teaching
Involvement of parents	Classrooms

> The heart and soul of school culture is what people believe, the assumptions they make about how school works.
>
> *Thomas Sergiovanni*

Here's how your journal entry might begin if you chose "Age of students":

"The ages of students at my high school ranged from about 14 to 18 years old. Here in college the ages of students range from about 17 to 40 or even older. In my math class this semester, I have a mother and daughter who are taking the class together. Overall, students here in college seem to average about 10 years older than students in high school. A couple of the older students that I've talked with went to college before and dropped out. These students seem to take their schoolwork more seriously than the younger students. They hardly ever miss a class or fail to turn in homework."

Becoming an Active Learner

Focus Questions How does the human brain learn? How can you use this knowledge to develop a highly effective system for learning?

Successful athletes understand how to get the most out of their physical abilities. Likewise, to be a successful learner, you need to know how to get the most out of your mental abilities. Much has been discovered, especially in the last few decades, about how human beings learn. To benefit from these discoveries, let's take a quick peek into our brains.

HOW THE HUMAN BRAIN LEARNS

The human brain weighs about three pounds and is composed of trillions of cells. About 100 billion of them are neurons, and here's where much of our learning takes place. When a potential learning experience occurs (such as reading this sentence), some neurons send out spikes of electrical activity. This activity causes nearby neurons to do the same. When neurons fire together, they form what is called a "neural network." I like to picture a bunch of neurons joining hands in my brain, jumping up and down, and having a learning party. If this party happens only once, learning is weak (as when you see your instructor solve a math problem one day and can't recall how to do it the next). However, if you cause the same collection of neurons to fire repeatedly (as when you solve 10 similar math problems yourself), the result is likely a long-term memory. According to David Sousa, author of *How the Brain Learns,* "Eventually, repeated firing of the pattern binds the neurons together so that if one fires, they all fire, ultimately forming a new memory trace."

> The human brain has the largest area of uncommitted cortex (no particular required function) of any species on earth. This gives humans extraordinary flexibility and capacity for learning.
>
> *Eric Jensen*

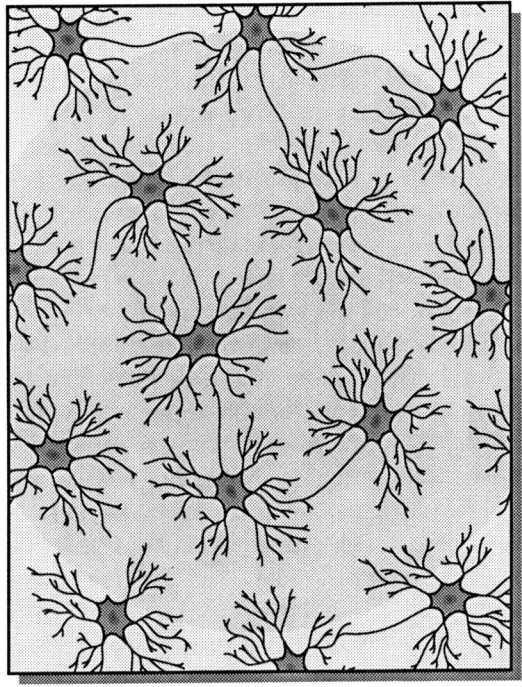
Neurons before learning.

Neurons after learning.

In other words, if you want learning to stick, you need to create strong neural networks. In this way, learning literally changes the structure of your brain. Through autopsies, neuroscientist Robert Jacobs and his colleagues determined that graduate students actually had 40 percent more neural connections than those of high school dropouts. Jacobs's research joins many other brain studies to reveal an important fact: **To excel as a learner, you need to create as many neural connections in your brain as possible.**

THREE PRINCIPLES OF DEEP AND LASTING LEARNING

With this brief introduction to what goes on in our brains, let's explore how highly effective learners maximize their learning. Whether they know it or not, they have figured out how to create many strong neural connections in their brains. And you can, too.

How? The short answer is: **Become an active learner**. Learning isn't a spectator sport. You don't create deep and lasting learning by passively listening to a lecture, casually skimming a textbook, or having a tutor solve math problems for you. In order to create strong neural networks, you've got to participate actively in the learning process.

Now, here's the longer answer. Good learners, consciously or unconsciously, implement three principles for creating deep and lasting learning:

> In a time of drastic change, it is the learners who inherit the future.
>
> *Eric Hoffer*

> When information goes "in one ear and out the other," it's often because it doesn't have anything to stick to.
>
> *Joshua Foer*

1. **PRIOR LEARNING.** Brain research reveals that when you connect what you are learning now to previously stored information (i.e., already-formed neural networks), you learn the new information or skill faster and more deeply. For example, the first word-processing program I learned was Word Perfect. It took me a long time to learn because I had no prior knowledge about word processing; thus, my brain contained few, if any, neural networks relevant to what I was learning. First, I needed to learn what word processing can do (such as delete whole paragraphs) and then I needed to learn how to perform that function with Word Perfect. Later, when I was learning another word-processing program, Microsoft Word, I already knew what word processing can do, so I was able to learn this new program in a fraction of the time. Put another way, I already had neural networks in my brain related to word processing, and learning Microsoft Word got those neurons partying.

    The contribution of past learning to new learning helps explain why some learners have difficulty in college with academic skills such as math, reading, and writing. If their earlier learning was shaky, they're going to have difficulty with new learning. They don't have strong neural networks on which to attach the new learning. It's like trying to construct a house on a weak foundation. In such a situation, the best option is to go back and strengthen the foundation, which is exactly the purpose of developmental (basic skills) courses. However, there's no point trying to learn these foundational skills the same way you learned them before. After all, how you learned them before didn't make the information or skills stick. So this time you'll need to employ different, more effective learning strategies, ones that will create the needed neural networks. If that's your situation, this time you'll have the advantage of employing the more effective strategies described here in *On Course*. And if you're a learner with a strong foundation, you'll find strategies here that will increase your effectiveness as a learner even more.

> Mathematics teachers... see students using a certain formula to solve problems correctly one day, but they cannot remember how to do it the next day. If the process was not stored, the information is treated as brand new again!
>
> *David A. Sousa*

2. **QUALITY OF PROCESSING.** How you exercise affects your physical strength. Likewise, how you study affects the strength of your neural networks and therefore the quality of your learning. Some information (such as math formulas or anatomy terms) must be recalled exactly as presented. For such learning tasks, effective memorization strategies are the types of processing that work best. However, much of what you'll be asked to learn in college is too complex for mere memorization (though many struggling students try). For mastering complex information and skills, you'll want to use what learning experts call **deep processing**. These are the very strategies that successful learners use to maximize their learning and make it stick. You'll learn both effective memorization and deep-processing strategies in the "Wise Choices in College" sections in later chapters.

Don't use just one deep-processing strategy, however. Successful athletes know the value of cross training, so they use a variety of training strategies. Similarly, successful learners know the value of employing *varied* deep-processing strategies. That's because the more ways you deep-process new learning, the stronger your neural networks become.

When you actively study any information or skill using *numerous and varied deep-processing strategies,* you create and strengthen related neural networks and your learning soars.

3. **QUANTITY OF PROCESSING.** The quality of your learning is significantly affected by how often and how long you engage in varied deep processing. This factor is often called "time on task," and the most effective approach is *distributed practice*. The human brain learns best when learning efforts are distributed over time. No successful athlete waits until the night before a competition to begin training. Why, then, do struggling students think they can start studying the night before a test? An all-night cram session may make a deposit in their short-term memories, perhaps even allowing them to pass a test the next day. However, even students who got good grades have experienced the ineffectiveness of cramming when they encounter "summer amnesia"—the inability to remember in fall-term classes what they learned during the previous school year. That's the result of not creating strong neural networks that make learning last. To create strong neural networks, you need to process the target information or skill with numerous and varied deep-processing strategies and do it *frequently*.

In addition to how frequently you use deep-processing strategies, also important is the *amount of time* you spend learning. Obviously, deep processing for 60 minutes generates more learning than deep processing for 5 minutes. So, highly effective learners put in **sufficient time on task.** The traditional guideline for a week's studying is two hours for each hour of class time. Thus, if you have 15 hours of classes per week, the estimate for your "sufficient time on task" is about 30 hours per week. Many struggling students neither study very often nor very long. However, some fool themselves by putting in "sufficient time," but spend little of it engaged in effective learning activities. They skim complex information in their textbooks. They attempt to memorize information they don't understand. Their minds wander to a conversation they had at lunch. They rummage through their book bags and dresser drawers and closets looking

Almost everyone has had occasion to look back upon his school days and wonder what has become of the knowledge he was supposed to have amassed during his days of schooling.

John Dewey

Three Principles of Deep and Lasting Learning

1. **Prior Learning.** Relate new information to previously learned information.
2. **Quality of Processing.** Use numerous and varied deep-processing strategies.
3. **Quantity of Processing.** Use frequent practice sessions of sufficient length distributed over time.

> Good learners, like everyone else, are living, squirming, questioning, perceiving, fearing, loving, and languaging nervous systems, but they are good learners precisely because they believe and do certain things that less effective learners do not believe and do. And therein lies the key.
>
> *Neil Postman
> & Charles Weingartner*

for their class notes. They play a video game or two. They phone a classmate. They send a couple of text messages, and the next thing they know, it's time to go to bed. When they fail the test the next day, they complain, "But I studied *so long*!"

Some students have a chemical imbalance that prevents them from focusing for long periods of time and their learning suffers. If you think this may be true for you, make an appointment with your college's disability counselor to get help. But the reason most students struggle with learning is fully within their control. You don't need a genius IQ to be a good learner and do well in college. What you do need is a learning system that employs what we now know about how the human brain learns. Billions of neurons between your ears are ready to party. Let the festival of learning begin!

THE CORE LEARNING SYSTEM

Four general strategies are common to good learners. To remember these strategies, simply think of the word CORE (see Figure 1.2). CORE stands for **Collect, Organize, Rehearse,** and **Evaluate.** The CORE learning system is effective because it automatically guides you to implement all three of the active learning principles discussed earlier. Thus, by applying what we know about how the human brain learns, the CORE learning system helps you create deep and lasting learning. Here's how it works:

Collect: In every waking moment, we're constantly collecting perceptions through our five senses. Without conscious effort, the brain takes in a multitude of sights, sounds, smells, tastes, and physical sensations. Most perceptions disappear within moments. Some, such as our first language, stick for a lifetime. Thus, much of what we learn in life we do without intention. In college, however, learning needs to be more conscious. That's because instructors expect you to learn specific information and skills. Then, of course, they want you to demonstrate that knowledge on quizzes, tests, exams, term papers, and other forms of evaluation. In college, two of the most important ways you'll collect information and skills are through reading textbooks and attending classes. In Chapters 2 and 3, you'll learn proven strategies for maximizing the amount of high-quality information you collect in these ways.

Organize: Once we collect information, we need to make sense of it. When learning in everyday life, we tend to organize collected information in unconscious ways. We don't even realize that we're doing it. However, in a college course, you need to organize information systematically so it makes sense to you. In fact, making meaning from collected information is one of the most important outcomes of studying.

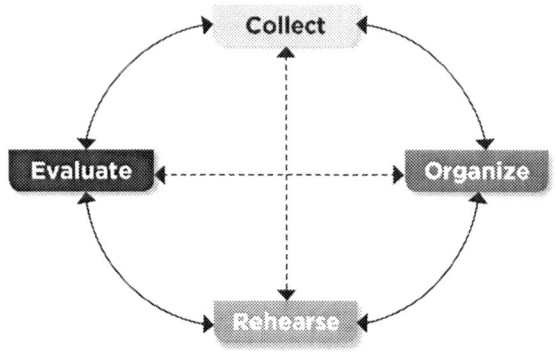

Figure 1.2 The CORE Learning System

In Chapters 4, 5, and 6, you'll learn proven strategies for organizing information into study materials that will lead to deep learning.

Rehearse: Once we collect and organize our target knowledge, we need to remember it for future use. Rehearsing (also called "practicing") strengthens neural networks and makes learning stick. When you solve 10 challenging math problems, you're rehearsing. Over time, the process of solving becomes easier and more natural. In Chapters 4, 5, and 6, you'll learn proven ways to rehearse information and skills so you can remember them for future use, whether on a test, in your career, or in your personal life.

Evaluate: Life is great at giving us informal feedback about the quality of our learning. Maybe you tell a joke and forget the punch line. You know immediately you have more learning to do. Higher education, however, provides us with more formal feedback. Yup, those pesky tests, term papers, quizzes, lab reports, essays, classroom questions, and final exams. Evaluation, both informal and formal, is an essential component of all learning because without feedback, we can never be sure if our learning is accurate or complete. Chapters 6 and 7 provide you with proven ways to assess what you have learned in your courses. Then you'll discover how to demonstrate that learning to instructors so you can maximize your grades in college.

Learning doesn't occur in a tidy, step-by-step fashion. At any moment while learning, you may need to jump to a different component in the CORE system. For example, while **Rehearsing,** you might realize that some information doesn't make sense to you, so you **Organize** it in a different way. At times you may engage two or more components simultaneously. For instance, when **Rehearsing** study materials, you're probably **Evaluating** your mastery of that knowledge at the same time. Thus, you can expect to use the four components of the CORE Learning System in any order and in any combination.

Although the CORE system is an effective blueprint for creating deep and lasting learning, not all learners prefer to **Collect, Organize, Rehearse,** and **Evaluate** in the same way. That's why you'll encounter many specific strategies in *On Course*. Your task is to experiment with and find the ones that work best for you. What you'll ultimately construct is a personalized learning system, one you can use for the rest of your life. In this way, you can be confident of your ability to learn anything you need to know on the path to achieving your goals and dreams in college and beyond.

> When something is meaningful it is organized; when it is organized, it is simplified in the mind.
>
> *Robert Ornstein*

> Education which strengthens a person's ability to gather, organize and evaluate information, contributes to more accurate adult judgments.
>
> *Muriel James & Dorothy Joneward*

▸ BELIEVING IN YOURSELF

Develop Self-Acceptance

 **Focus Questions** Why is high self-esteem so important to success? What can you do to raise your self-esteem?

Roland was in his 40's when he enrolled in my English 101 class. He made insightful contributions to class discussions, so I was perplexed when the first two writing assignments passed without an essay from Roland. Both times, he apologized profusely, promising to complete them soon. He didn't want to make excuses, he said, but he was stretched to his limit: He worked at night, and during the day he took care of his two young sons while his wife worked. "Don't worry, though," he assured me, "I'll have an essay to you by Monday. I'm going to be the first person in my family to get a college degree. Nothing's going to stop me."

But Monday came, and Roland was absent. On a hunch, I looked up his academic record and found that he had taken English 101 twice before. I contacted his previous instructors. Both of them said that Roland had made many promises but had never turned in an assignment.

I called Roland, and we made an appointment to talk. He didn't show up. During the next class, I invited Roland into the hall while the class was working on a writing assignment.

"Sorry I missed our conference," Roland said. "I meant to call, but things have been piling up."

"Roland, I talked to your other instructors, and I know you never wrote anything for them. I'd love to help you, but you need to take an action. You need to write an essay." Roland nodded silently. "I believe you can do it. But I don't know if *you* believe you can do it. It's decision time. What do you say?"

"I'll have an essay to you by Friday."

I looked him in the eye.

"Promise," he said.

I knew that what Roland actually did, not what he promised, would reveal his deepest core beliefs about himself.

SELF-ESTEEM AND CORE BELIEFS

So it is with us all. Our core beliefs—true or false, real or imagined—form the inner compass that guides our choices.

At the heart of our core beliefs is the statement *I AM ___*. How we complete that sentence in the quiet of our souls has a profound effect on the quality of our lives.

The foundation of anyone's ability to cope successfully is high self-esteem. If you don't already have it, you can always develop it.

Virginia Satir

Self-esteem is the reputation we have with ourselves.

Nathaniel Branden

High self-esteem is the fuel that can propel us into the cycle of success. Do we approve of ourselves as we are, accepting our personal weaknesses along with our strengths? Do we believe ourselves capable, admirable, lovable, and fully worthy of the best life has to offer? If so, our beliefs will make it possible for us to choose wisely and stay on course to a rich, full life.

For example, imagine two students: one with high self-esteem, the other with low self-esteem. Picture them just after they get very disappointing test scores. What do they do next? The student with low self-esteem will likely choose options that protect his fragile self-image, options such as dropping the course rather than chancing failure. The student with high self-esteem, on the other hand, will likely choose options that move her toward success, options such as persisting in the course and getting additional help to be successful. Two students, same situation. One focuses on weaknesses. One focuses on strengths. The result: two different choices and two very different outcomes.

The good news is that self-esteem is learned, so anyone can learn to raise his or her self-esteem. Much of this book is about how you can do just that.

> Self-esteem is more than merely recognizing one's positive qualities. It is an attitude of acceptance and non-judgment toward self and others.
>
> *Matthew McKay & Patrick Fanning*

KNOW AND ACCEPT YOURSELF

People with high self-esteem know that no one is perfect, and they accept themselves with both their strengths and weaknesses. To paraphrase philosopher Reinhold Niebuhr, successful people accept the things they cannot change, have the courage to change the things they can change, and possess the wisdom to know the difference.

Successful people have the courage to take an honest self-inventory, as you began doing in Journal Entry 1. They acknowledge their strengths without false humility, and they admit their weaknesses without stubborn denial. They tell the truth about themselves and take action to improve what they can.

Fortunately for Roland, he decided to do just that. On the Friday after our talk, he turned in his English 101 essay. His writing showed great promise, and I told him so. I also told him I appreciated that he had let go of the excuse that he was too busy to do his assignments. From then on, Roland handed in his essays on time. He met with me in conferences. He visited the writing lab, and he did grammar exercises to improve his editing skills. He easily passed the course.

A few years later, Roland called me. He had transferred to a four-year university and was graduating with a 3.8 average. He was continuing on to

AS SMART AS HE WAS, ALBERT EINSTEIN COULD NOT FIGURE OUT HOW TO HANDLE THOSE TRICKY BOUNCES AT THIRD BASE.

> We cannot change anything unless we accept it.
>
> *Carl Jung*

graduate school to study urban planning. What he most wanted me to know was that one of his instructors had asked permission to use one of his essays as a model of excellent writing. "You know," Roland said, "I'd still be avoiding writing if I hadn't accepted two things about myself: I was a little bit lazy and I was a whole lot scared. Once I admitted those things about myself, I started changing."

Each of us has a unique combination of strengths and weaknesses. When struggling people become aware of a weakness, they typically blame the problem on others or they beat themselves up for not being perfect. Successful people, however, usually make a different choice: They acknowledge the weakness, accept it without self-judgment, and, when possible, take action to create positive changes. As always, the choices we make determine both where we are headed and the quality of the journey. Developing self-acceptance helps us to make those choices wisely.

> Be what you is, not what you ain't, 'cause if you ain't what you is, you is what you ain't.
>
> *Luther D. Price*

Journal Entry 4

In this activity, you will explore your strengths and weaknesses and the reputation you have with yourself. This exploration of your self-esteem will allow you to begin revising any limiting beliefs you may hold about yourself. By doing so, you will take a major step toward your success.

1. **In your journal, write a list of 10 or more of your personal strengths.** For example, mentally: *I'm good at math;* physically: *I'm very athletic;* emotionally: *I seldom let anger control me;* socially: *I'm a good friend;* and others: *I am almost always on time.*

2. **Write a list of 10 or more of your personal weaknesses.** For example, mentally: *I'm a slow reader;* physically: *I am out of shape;* emotionally: *I'm easily hurt by criticism;* socially: *I don't listen very well;* and others: *I'm a terrible procrastinator.*

3. **Using the information in Steps 1 and 2 and score #8 on your self-assessment, write about the present state of your self-esteem.** On a scale of 1 to 10 (with 10 high), how strong is your self-esteem? How do you think it got to be that way? How would you like it to be? What changes could you make to achieve your ideal self-esteem?

To create an outstanding journal, remember to use the five suggestions printed on the inside back cover of *On Course*. Especially remember to dive deep!

Adopting a Creator Mindset

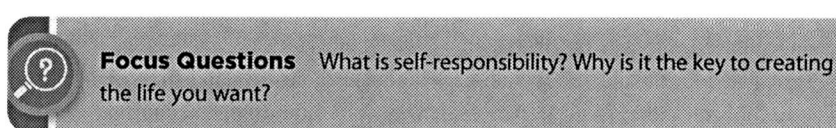

Focus Questions What is self-responsibility? Why is it the key to creating the life you want?

When psychologist Richard Logan studied people who survived ordeals such as being imprisoned in concentration camps or lost in the frozen Arctic, he found they shared a common belief. They all saw themselves as personally responsible for creating the outcomes and experiences of their lives.

Ironically, responsibility has gotten a bad reputation. Some see it as a heavy burden they have to lug through life. Quite the contrary, personal responsibility is the foundation for creating success. Personal *response-ability* is the ability to respond wisely at each fork in the road, your choices moving you ever closer to your desired outcomes and experiences. The opposite is waiting passively for your fate to be determined by luck or powerful others. Whether your challenge is surviving an Arctic blizzard or excelling in college, accepting personal responsibility empowers you to make the most out of any situation.

I first met Deborah when she was a student in my English 101 class. Deborah wanted to be a nurse, but before she could qualify for the nursing program, she had to pass English 101. She was taking the course for the fourth time.

"Your writing shows fine potential," I told Deborah after I had read her first essay. "You'll pass English 101 as soon as you eliminate your grammar problems."

"I know," she said. "That's what my other three instructors said."

"Well, let's make this your last semester in English 101, then. After each essay, make an appointment with me to go over your grammar problems."

"Okay."

"And go to the Writing Lab as often as possible. Start by studying verb tense. Let's eliminate one problem at a time."

"I'll go this afternoon!"

But Deborah never found time: *No, really. . . . I'll go to the lab just as soon as I. . . .*

Deborah scheduled two appointments with me during the semester and missed them both: *I'm so sorry. . . . I'll come to see you just as soon as I. . . .*

To pass English 101 at our college, students had to pass one of two essays written at the end of the semester in an exam setting. Each essay, identified by social security number only, was graded by two other instructors. At semester's end, Deborah once again failed English 101. "It isn't fair!" Deborah protested. "Those exam graders expect us to be professional writers. They're keeping me from becoming a nurse!"

I suggested another possibility: "What if *you* are the one keeping you from becoming a nurse?"

> The best years of your life are the ones in which you decide your problems are your own. You do not blame them on your mother, the ecology, or the president. You realize that you control your own destiny.
>
> *Albert Ellis*

> The more we practice the habit of acting from a position of responsibility, the more effective we become as human beings, and the more successful we become as managers of our lives.
>
> *Joyce Chapman*

Deborah didn't like that idea. She wanted to believe that her problem was "out there." Her only obstacle was *those* exam graders. All her disappointments were *their* fault. *They* weren't fair. The *test* wasn't fair. *Life* wasn't fair! In the face of this injustice, she was helpless.

I reminded Deborah that it was *she* who had not studied her grammar. It was *she* who had not come to conferences. It was *she* who had not accepted personal responsibility for creating her life the way she wanted it.

"Yes, but …," she said.

VICTIM AND CREATOR MINDSETS

Deborah had a problem that was going to keep her from ever passing English 101. But the problem wasn't the exam graders. The problem was her mindset.

A mindset is a collection of beliefs and attitudes. Like a lens, it affects the way you see a situation and influences your resulting choices. A **Victim mindset** keeps people from seeing and acting on choices that could help them achieve the life they want. A **Creator mindset** causes people to see multiple options, choose wisely among them, and take effective actions to achieve the life they want.

When you accept personal responsibility, you believe that you create *everything* in your life. This idea doesn't sit well with some people. "Accidents and natural disasters happen," they say. "There are muggings, murders, and wars. People are marginalized, oppressed, and brutalized simply because they are different. Blaming the victims is unfair. To say these people created the terrible things that happened to them is outrageous."

These observations are, as far as they go, true. At times, we *are* all affected by forces beyond our control. If a hurricane destroys my house, I am a victim (with a small "v"). In this case I am victimized by a force *outside* of me. But if I allow that event to ruin my life, I am a Victim (with a capital "V"). In this case I am victimized by a force *inside* of me. Whether I am victimized from the outside or from the inside is a crucial distinction. When I have a Victim mindset, I become my own oppressor. When I have a Creator mindset, I refuse to be oppressed.

Civil rights activist Rosa Parks is a perfect example of this distinction. On the evening of December 1, 1955, Parks was returning home on a Montgomery, Alabama, bus. She had just completed a long day as a seamstress in a department store. When the driver ordered her to give up her seat to a white passenger, Parks refused and was arrested. A few days later, outraged at her arrest, African Americans began a boycott of Montgomery buses that ended 381 days later when the law requiring segregation on public buses was finally lifted. As a result of choosing defiance, Parks has been called the "mother of the modern day civil rights movement." In an interview years later, Parks was asked why she choose to defy the bus driver's order to move. "People always say that I didn't give up my seat because I was tired," she said, "but that isn't true. I was not tired physically, or no more tired than I usually was at the end of a working day. I was not old, although some people have an image of me as being old then.

Every time your back is against the wall, there is only one person that can help. And that's you. It has to come from inside.

Pat Riley, professional basketball coach

Which mistake do you think would be better to make . . . a) to believe you are in control of your life when you really might not be [or] b) to believe you are not in control of your life when you really might be?

Brooks Peterson

I was forty-two. No, the only tired I was, was tired of giving in." In the face of an external oppression, Rosa Parks became an inspiring example of what one person with a Creator mindset can achieve.

So, is it outrageous to believe that you create everything in your life? Of course it is. But here's a better question: Would it improve your life to act *as if* you create all of the outcomes and experiences in your life? Answer "YES!" and watch a Creator mindset improve your life. After all, if you believe that someone or something out there causes all of your problems, then it's up to "them" to change. What a wait that can be! How long, for example, will Deborah have to wait for "those exam graders" to change?

The benefits to students of accepting personal responsibility have been demonstrated in various studies. Researchers Robert Vallerand and Robert Bissonette, for example, asked 1,000 first-year college students to complete a questionnaire about why they were attending school. They used the students' answers to assess whether the students were "Origin-like" or "Pawn-like." The researchers defined *Origin-like* students as seeing themselves as the originators of their own behaviors, in other words, Creators. By contrast, *Pawn-like* students see themselves as mere puppets controlled by others, in other words, Victims. A year later, the researchers returned to find out what had happened to the 1,000 students. They found that significantly more of the Creator-like students were still enrolled in college than the Victim-like students. If you want to succeed in college (and in life), having a Creator mindset gives you a big edge.

> I believe that we are solely responsible for our choices, and we have to accept the consequences of every deed, word, and thought throughout our lifetime.
>
> *Elisabeth Kübler-Ross*

RESPONSIBILITY AND CULTURE

In the 1950s, American psychologist Julian Rotter set out to study people's beliefs about who or what was responsible for the outcomes and experiences of their lives. He called it a study of "locus of control." *Locus* in Latin means "place" or "location." So, "locus of control" defines where people believe the power over their lives is located. Since Rotter's study, locus of control has been one of the

most examined aspects of human nature. What researchers discovered is that different cultures see locus of control differently.

People of some cultures believe they control their own destiny. Researchers call this mindset an *internal* locus of control. People with this mindset believe their outcomes and experiences depend on their own behaviors. This mindset is part of North American culture, where maturity is often defined as taking responsibility for one's own life. Not surprisingly, a strong part of the deep culture of North American higher education is a belief that college students are adults. As such, students are expected to make adult choices and be willing to accept responsibility for the consequences of those choices.

However, researchers found that people from some cultures assign responsibility for their fate to factors beyond their control. If you find that you are uncomfortable with the idea of personal responsibility, the cause may be found in your deep culture. For example, members of Latino culture, with roots in Catholicism, are likely to believe that a higher power is guiding their lives. The saying *Si Dios Quiere* ("If God Wants") reflects this belief. Muslims have a similar phrase in Arabic: *Insha'Allah* means "God willing" or "if God allows." Traditional Native Americans also value fate over self-determination. And members of working-class cultures—regardless of their ethnicity—may experience economic frustrations and doubt their ability to create the life of their dreams.

These differences in cultural mindsets highlight both the challenge and importance of deciding where our responsibilities begin and end. On the one hand, accepting too little responsibility is disempowering. We become little more than a feather floating on the breeze. On the other hand, accepting too much responsibility is disempowering as well. In some cases, we become like a pack mule crushed under the weight of problems not of our creation or in our control. The reality is that some choices truly are futile because of personal limitations or limitations imposed by fate or the will of others with more power. Like some kind of cosmic joke, one of our greatest responsibilities, then, is deciding what we are and are not responsible for, what we do and do not have control over. Worse, those decisions may change at the very next fork in the road. As a guideline to help you choose, in North American culture you'll usually be wise to adopt the philosophy of English poet William E. Henley, who in 1875 wrote: "I am the master of my fate; I am the captain of my soul." In fact, had Henley been a college student at the time, he might have added, "And I am the Creator of my GPA."

RESPONSIBILITY AND CHOICE

The key ingredient of personal responsibility is **choice.** Animals respond to a stimulus because of instinct or habit. For humans, however, there is a brief, critical moment of decision available between the stimulus and the response. In this moment, we make the choices—consciously or unconsciously—that influence the outcomes of our lives.

Numerous times each day, you come to a fork in the road and must make a choice. Even *not* making a choice is a choice. Some choices have a small impact: Shall I get my hair cut today or tomorrow? Some have a huge impact: Shall

---

Generally, European-American teachers believe in internal control and internal responsibility—that individuals are in control of their own fate, their actions affect outcomes, and success or failure in life is related to personal characteristics and abilities.

Jean Moule

By imposing too great a responsibility, or rather, all responsibility, on yourself, you crush yourself.

Franz Kafka

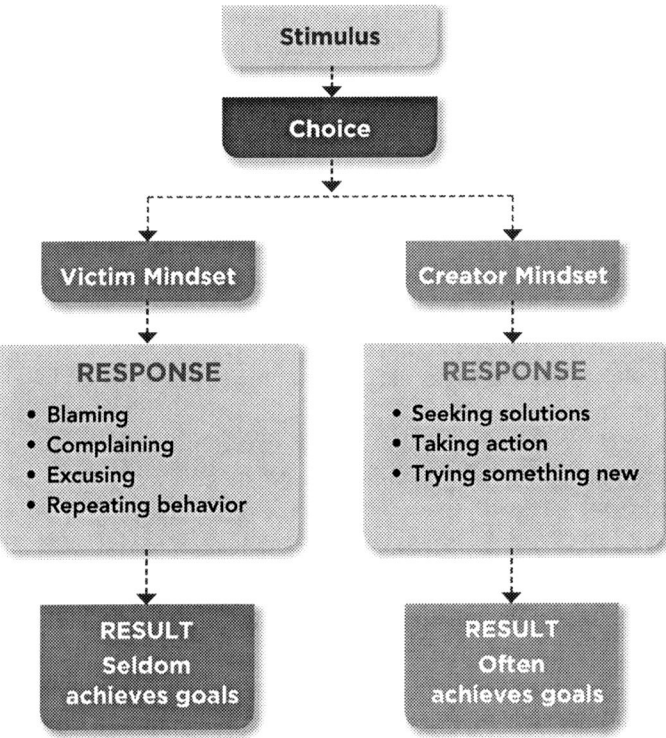

Figure 2.1 Responsibility Model

> I do think that the greatest lesson of life is that you are responsible for your own life.
>
> *Oprah Winfrey*

I stay in college or drop out? The sum of the choices you make from this day forward will create the eventual outcome of your life. The Responsibility Model in Figure 2.1 shows what the moment of choice looks like.

In that brief moment between stimulus and response, we can choose a Victim mindset or a Creator mindset. When we respond as a Victim, we typically complain, blame, make excuses, and then repeat ineffective behaviors. When we respond as a Creator, we pause at each decision point and ask, "What are my options, and which option will best help me create my desired outcomes and experiences?"

The difference between responding to life as a Victim or Creator is how we choose to use our energy. When I'm blaming, complaining, and excusing, my efforts cause little or no improvement. Sure, it may feel good in that moment to claim that I'm a poor Victim and "they" are evil persecutors, but my good feelings are fleeting because afterward my problem still exists. By contrast, when I'm seeking solutions and taking actions, my efforts often (though not always) lead to improvements. At critical forks in the road, Victims waste their energy and remain stuck, whereas Creators use their energy for improving their lives. There is only one situation I can think of where blaming and complaining can be helpful. That's when you use them to generate energy that motivates you to take positive actions. My personal guideline: Up to 10 minutes for griping . . . then on to being a Creator and finding a solution.

> When you make the shift to being the predominant creative force in your life, you move from reacting and responding to the external circumstances of your life to creating directly the life you truly want.
>
> *Robert Fritz*

But, let's be honest. No one makes Creator choices all of the time. I've never met anyone who did, least of all me. Our inner lives feature a perpetual tug of war between the Creator part of us and the Victim part of us. My own experiences have taught me the following life lesson: The more choices I make as a Creator, the more I improve the quality of my life. That's why I urge you to join me in an effort to choose more often as a Creator. It won't be easy, but it's worth it. You may have to take my word for it right now, but if you experiment with the strategies in this book and continue using the ones that work for you, in a few months you'll see powerful proof in your own life of the value of making Creator choices.

"Oh, I get what you mean!" one of my students once exclaimed as we were exploring this complex issue of personal responsibility, "You're saying that living my life is like traveling in my car. If I want to get where I want to go, I better be the driver and not a passenger."

She was right. Personal responsibility is about taking hold of the steering wheel of our lives, about taking control of where we go and how we get there. Ultimately, each of us creates the quality of our life with the wisdom or folly of our choices.

> I am a Shawnee. My forefathers were warriors. Their son is a warrior.... From my tribe I take nothing. I am the maker of my own fortune.
>
> *Tecumseh*

> Life is like a game of cards. The hand you are dealt is determinism; the way you play it is free will.
>
> *Jawaharlal Nehru*

Journal Entry 5

In this activity, you will experiment with the Creator role. By choosing to take responsibility for your life, you will immediately gain an increased power to achieve your greatest potential.

1. **Write and complete each of the five sentence stems below.** For example, someone might complete the first sentence stem as follows: *If I take personal responsibility for my education, I will focus on really learning and not just getting good grades.*

   1. If I take personal responsibility for my education . . .
   2. If I take personal responsibility for my career . . .
   3. If I take personal responsibility for my relationships . . .
   4. If I take personal responsibility for my health . . .
   5. If I take personal responsibility for all that happens to me . . .

2. **Make a choice: Write about one of the following:**

   A. **What have you learned or relearned in this journal about personal responsibility, and how you will use this knowledge to improve your outcomes and experiences in college . . . and beyond?** If you are aware that accepting personal responsibility conflicts with your own cultural or personal beliefs, explore how you will deal with that difference. You might begin, *By reading and writing about personal responsibility, I have learned . . .*

   B. **Share the details of a personal experience in which you did or did not take personal responsibility and explain the effects of this choice on your life.**

BELIEVING IN YOURSELF

Change Your Inner Conversation

 **Focus Question** How can you raise your self-esteem by changing your self-talk?

Imagine this: Three students schedule an appointment with their instructor to discuss a project they're working on together. They go to the instructor's office at the scheduled time, but he isn't there. They wait 45 minutes before leaving. As you learn what they do next, which student do you think has the strongest self-esteem?

Student 1, feeling discouraged and depressed, spends the evening watching television while neglecting assignments in other subjects. Student 2, feeling insulted and furious, spends the evening complaining to friends about the horrible instructor who stood them up. Student 3, feeling puzzled about the mix-up, emails the instructor to see what happened and to set up another meeting; while waiting for a response, this student spends the evening studying for a test in another class.

Which student has the strongest self-esteem?

THE CURSE OF STINKIN' THINKIN'

How is it that three people can have the same experience and respond to it so differently? According to psychologists like Albert Ellis, the answer lies in what each person believes caused the event. Ellis suggested that different responses can be understood by realizing that the activating event (A) plus our beliefs (B) equal the consequences (C) (how we respond). In other words, A + B = C. For example:

Activating Event	+ Beliefs	= Consequence
Student #1: Instructor didn't show up for a scheduled conference.	My instructor thinks I'm dumb. I'll never get a college degree. I'm a failure in life.	Got depressed and watched television all evening.
Student #2: Same.	My instructor won't help me. Teachers don't care about students.	Got angry and spent the night telling friends how horrible the instructor is.
Student #3: Same.	I'm not sure what went wrong. Sometimes things just don't turn out the way you plan. There's always tomorrow.	Emailed the instructor to see what happened and to set up a new appointment; then studied for another class.

> It is the mind that maketh good or ill, That maketh wretch or happy, rich or poor.
>
> *Edmund Spencer*

> Self-esteem can be defined as the state that exists when you are not arbitrarily haranguing and abusing yourself but choose to fight back against those automatic thoughts with meaningful rational responses.
>
> *Dr. Thomas Burns*

Ellis suggests that our upsets are caused not so much by our problems as by what we *think* about our problems. When our thinking is full of irrational beliefs—what Ellis calls "stinkin' thinkin'"—we feel awful even when the circumstances don't warrant it. So, how we *think* about the events in our lives is the key issue. Problems may come and go, but our "stinkin' thinkin'" stays with us. As the old saying goes, "Everywhere I go, there I am."

Stinkin' thinkin' isn't based on reality. Rather, these irrational thoughts are the automatic chatter of the Inner Critic (keeper of Negative Beliefs about the self) and the Inner Defender (keeper of Negative Beliefs about other people and the world).

So what about our three students and their self-esteem? It's not hard to see that student 1, who got depressed and wasted the evening watching television, has low self-esteem. This student is thrown far off course simply by the instructor's not showing up. A major cause of this self-defeating reaction is the Inner Critic's harsh self-judgments. Here are some common self-damning beliefs held by Inner Critics:

> The Inner Critic keeps us feeling insecure and childlike. When it is operating, we feel like children who have done something wrong and probably will never be able to do anything right.
>
> *Hal Stone & Sidra Stone*

I'm dumb.   I'm unattractive.
I'm selfish.   I'm lazy.
I'm a failure.   I'm not college material
I'm incapable.   I'm weak.
I'm not as good as other people.   I'm a lousy parent.
I'm worthless.   I'm unlovable.

People dominated by their Inner Critic often misinterpret events, inventing criticisms that aren't there. A friend says, "Something came up, and I can't meet you tonight." The Inner Critic responds, "I screwed up again! I'll never have any friends!"

The activating event doesn't cause the consequence; rather, the judgmental chatter of the Inner Critic does. A strong Inner Critic is both a cause and an effect of low self-esteem.

What about student 2, the one who spent the evening telling friends how horrible the instructor was? Though perhaps less apparent, this student's judgmental response also demonstrates low self-esteem. The finger-pointing Inner Defender is merely the Inner Critic turned outward and is just as effective at getting the student off course. Here are some examples of destructive beliefs held by an Inner Defender:

> Everyone has a critical inner voice. But people with low self-esteem tend to have a more vicious and vocal pathological critic.
>
> *Matthew McKay & Patrick Fanning*

People don't treat me right, so they're rotten.
People don't act the way I want them to, so they're awful.
People don't live up to my expectations, so they're the enemy.
People don't do what I want, so they're against me.
Life is full of problems, so it's terrible.
Life is unfair, so I can't stand it.
Life doesn't always go my way, so I can't be happy.
Life doesn't provide me with everything I want, so it's unbearable.

People dominated by their Inner Defender imagine personal insults and slights in neutral events. A classmate says, "Something came up, and I can't meet you tonight." The Inner Defender responds, "Who do you think you are, anyway? I can find someone a lot better to study with than you!"

The activating event doesn't cause the angry response; rather, the judgmental chatter of the judgmental Inner Defender does. A strong Inner Defender is both a cause and an effect of low self-esteem.

Only student 3 demonstrates high self-esteem. This student realizes he doesn't know why the instructor missed the meeting. He doesn't blame himself, the instructor, or a rotten world. He considers alternatives: Perhaps the instructor got sick or was involved in a traffic accident. Until he finds out what happened and decides what to do next, this student turns his attention to an action that will keep him on course to another goal. The Inner Guide is concerned with positive results, not judging self or others. A strong Inner Guide is both a cause and an effect of high self-esteem.

DISPUTING IRRATIONAL BELIEFS

How, then, can you avoid stinkin' thinkin'?

First, you can become aware of the chatter of your Inner Critic and Inner Defender. Be especially alert when events in your life go wrong, when your desired outcomes and experiences are thwarted. That's when we are most likely to complain, blame, and excuse. That's when we substitute judgments of ourselves or others for the positive actions that would get us back on course.

Once you become familiar with your inner voices, you can begin a process of separating yourself from your Inner Critic and Inner Defender. To do this, practice disputing your irrational and self-sabotaging beliefs. Here are four effective ways to dispute:

- **Offer evidence that your judgments are incorrect:** *My instructor emailed me last week to see if I needed help with my project, so there's no rational reason to believe he won't help me now.*
- **Offer a positive explanation of the problem:** *Sure my instructor didn't show up, but he may have missed the appointment because of a last-minute crisis.*
- **Question the importance of the problem:** *Even if my instructor won't help me, I can still do well on this project, and if I don't, it won't be the end of the world.*
- **If you find that your judgments are true, instead of continuing to criticize yourself or someone else, offer a plan to improve the situation:** *If I'm honest, I have to admit that I haven't done well in this class so far, but from now on I'm going to attend every class, take good notes, read my assignments two or three times, and work with a study group before every test.*

According to psychologist Ellis, a key to correcting irrational thinking is changing a "must" into a preference. When we think "must," what follows in our thoughts is typically awful, terrible, and dreadful. For example, my Inner Defender's belief that an instructor "must" meet me for an appointment or he is an awful, terrible, dreadful person is irrational; I'd certainly "prefer" him to meet me for an

---

Replacing a negative thought with a positive one changes more than just the passing thought—it changes the way you perceive and deal with the world.

Dr. Clair Douglas

Does it help to change what you say to yourself? It most certainly does.... Tell yourself often enough that you'll succeed and you dramatically improve your chances of succeeding and of feeling good.

Drs. Bernie Zilbergeld & Arnold A. Lazarus

appointment, but his not meeting me does not make him horrible—in fact, he may have a perfectly good reason for not meeting with me. As another example, my Inner Critic's belief that I "must" pass this course or I am an awful, terrible, dreadful person is irrational; I'd certainly "prefer" to pass this course, but not doing so does not make me worthless—in fact, not passing this course may lead me to something even better. Believing irrationally that I, another person, or the world "must" be a particular way, Ellis says, is a major cause of my distress and misery.

STEREOTYPE THREAT

Social psychologist Claude Steele of Stanford University has identified a kind of stinkin' thinkin' that afflicts cultural groups: *stereotype threat*. A stereotype is a generalization about members of a particular group. For example, African Americans are all excellent in sports but they aren't good students . . . or women are all terrific at taking care of children but they are poor at math and science. Stereotype threat is a fear that your behavior in a particular situation—such as taking a math test—might confirm a negative stereotype about a cultural group to which you belong. The resulting anxiety causes a self-fulfilling prophesy, and you do, indeed, perform down to the stereotype rather than up to your ability.

As an example of the effect of stereotype threat, Steele and his colleagues showed that when race was emphasized, African-American college students did less well than their white classmates on a standardized test. However, when race was not emphasized, African-American students' scores were equivalent to those of white students. Further studies have shown that the academic success of many cultural groups fall prey to stereotype threat, including Latinos, females in math, and students of working-class backgrounds.

Here's how stinkin' thinkin' seems to contribute to stereotype threat. Let's say a female student sits down to take a math test. That's the activating event. Next come her beliefs: She knows the stereotype—women aren't good at math. She doesn't want to be lumped into or reinforce that stereotype. She becomes anxious, distracted, and can't remember all she studied. The result is a self-fulfilling prophesy. She doesn't do as well on the test as she is capable of, and the culprit is her stinkin' thinkin'.

Besides causing immediate problems in test situations, stereotype threat may even cause people to avoid the threat area altogether. A woman may avoid majoring in math and science. A white man may reject playing basketball. A working-class student may lose motivation and drop out of college.

The strategies for disputing that were mentioned earlier can also be applied to stereotype threat. A woman may **offer evidence that the stereotype is wrong**: *I did pretty well in math and science in high school . . . and I just read that four women recently won Nobel Prizes in science and mathematics.* A white man may **question the importance of the stereotype**: *I may not be the best player on the basketball team, but so what . . . it's great fun.* A working-class student may **offer a plan to address the stereotype**: *My English teacher told us her parents were migrant farm workers; I'm going to talk to her about how she kept herself motivated to get a college degree.*

Another way to reduce the negative impact of stereotype threat has been suggested by psychologists Michael Johns, Toni Schmader, and Andy Martens in a

---

You mainly make yourself needlessly and neurotically miserable by strongly holding absolutist irrational beliefs, especially by rigidly believing unconditional shoulds, oughts, and musts.

Albert Ellis

Everyone experiences stereotype threat. We are all members of some group about which negative stereotypes exist, from white males and Methodists to women and the elderly.

Claude M. Steele

study at the University of Arizona. They gave a math test to one group of students and found that female students performed worse than the men. Before giving the math test to a second group, they told students briefly about how stereotype threat could negatively affect the performance of women. Specifically, they announced, "It's important to keep in mind that if you are feeling anxious while taking this test, this anxiety could be the result of these negative stereotypes that are widely known in society and have nothing to do with your actual ability to do well on the test." In this second round of tests, female students did as well as the men. It seems that simply knowing about stereotype threat can reduce its power.

The guiding principle in this section is simple: Choose wisely the thoughts you allow to occupy your mind. Avoid letting automatic, negative thoughts or negative stereotypes undermine your self-esteem or your results. Evict stinkin' thinkin' and replace it with thoughts that empower.

Journal Entry 8

In this activity, you will practice disputing the judgments of your Inner Critic and your Inner Defender. As you become more skilled at seeing yourself, other people, and the world more objectively and without distracting judgments, your self-esteem will thrive.

1. **Write a sentence expressing a recent problem or event that upset you.** Think of something troubling that happened in school, at work, or in your personal life. For example, *I got a 62 on my math test.*

2. **Write a list of three or more criticisms your Inner Critic (IC) might level against you as a result of this situation. Have your Inner Guide (IG) dispute each one immediately.** Review the four methods of disputing described on page 65. You only need to use one of them for each criticism. For example,

    IC: You failed that math test because you're terrible in math.

    IG: It's true I failed the math test, but I'll study harder next time and do better. This was only the first test, and I now know what to expect next time.

3. **Write a list of three or more criticisms your Inner Defender (ID) might level against someone else or life as a result of this situation. Have your Inner Guide (IG) dispute each one immediately.** Again use one of the four methods for disputing. For example,

    ID: You failed that math test because you've got the worst math instructor on campus.

    IG: I have trouble understanding my math instructor, so I'm going to make an appointment to talk with him in private. John really liked him last semester, so I bet I'll like him, too, if I give him a chance.

Creating Inner Motivation

 **Focus Questions** How important do educators think motivation is to your academic success? What determines how motivated you are? What can you do to keep your motivation consistently high this semester ... and beyond?

Recently, two extensive surveys asked college and university educators to rank factors that hinder students' success and persistence. These surveys were done by American College Testing (ACT) and the Policy Center on the First Year of College. In both surveys, educators identified *lack of motivation* as the number one barrier to students' success in college.

> There are three things to remember about education. The first is motivation. The second is motivation. The third is motivation.
>
> Terrell Bell, former U.S. Secretary of Education

Lack of motivation has various symptoms: students arriving late to class or being absent, assignments turned in late or not at all, work done sloppily, appointments missed, offers of support ignored, and students not participating in class discussions or activities, to name just a few. But the most glaring symptom of all is the enormous number of students who vanish from college within their first year. According to ACT, about one-third of students in U.S. four-year public colleges and universities fail to return for their second year. In public two-year colleges, it's even worse: Nearly *half* of first-year students don't make it to a second year. Despite these grim statistics, you can be among those who stay and thrive in higher education!

A FORMULA FOR MOTIVATION

The study of human motivation—exploring why we do what we do—is extensive and complex. However, one formula explains much about academic motivation: $V \times E = M$.

In this formula, "V" stands for "value." In terms of your education, value is determined by the benefits you believe you'll obtain from seeking and obtaining a college degree. The greater the benefits you assign to college experiences and outcomes, the greater will be your motivation. The greater your motivation, the higher the cost you'll be willing to pay in terms of time, money, effort, frustration, inconvenience, and sacrifice. Take a moment to identify the score that presently represents the value you place on seeking and obtaining a college education. Choose a number from 0 to 10 (where "0" represents no perceived value and "10" represents an extremely high perceived value).

Having rated the value you place on achieving a college education, consider for a moment how your deep culture influenced your rating. Some cultural beliefs will boost your motivation, giving you staying power when the going gets rough. For example, most Chinese mothers place a high value on education, according to researcher Ruth K. Choa. They are quite willing to make big sacrifices to help their children succeed in school. Parents of middle- and upper-class students in North America are also known to place a high value on education. When parents in a culture demonstrate with words and deeds that they value education, the odds are great their children will as well.

Conversely, some cultures devalue formal education, thus lowering academic motivation. Working-class culture in North America often encourages its members to leave school in favor of a job and paycheck. Once the majority on campus, men now represent only about 43 percent of enrollment at North American colleges. It appears that to a growing number of men, "school is not cool." Some minorities, anthropologist John Ogbu observed, put little effort into academics in order to avoid the cultural stigma of acting "white." In a dominant culture that prizes education, such mindsets put members of these cultures in a painful dilemma. To do well in school goes against their culture, but to do poorly in school handicaps their future. Bottom line: To keep your motivation high, you'll need to have a clear sense of the personal value to you of a college degree.

In the formula $V \times E = M$, the "E" stands for "expectation." In terms of your education, expectation is determined by how likely you think it is that you can earn a college degree with a reasonable effort. To make that calculation, you need to weigh your abilities (how good a student you are and how strong your previous education is) against the difficulty of achieving your goal (how challenging the courses are that you will need to take and how much you are willing to sacrifice to be successful). Take a moment to identify the score that presently represents your personal expectation of being able to complete a college degree with a reasonable effort. Choose a number from 0 to 10 (where "0" represents no expectation of success and "10" represents an extremely high expectation of success).

> Today's theories about motivation emphasize the importance of factors within the individual, particularly the variables of expectancy and value. Students' motivations are strongly influenced by what they think is important (value) and what they believe they can accomplish (expectancy).
>
> *K. Patricia Cross*

> There is evidence that the time for learning various subjects would be cut to a fraction of the time currently allotted if the material were perceived by the learner as related to his own purposes.
>
> *Carl Rogers*

Once again, consider how cultural influences may have swayed your expectations of success in college. If your rating is high, consider whether your score reflects the expectation of your parents or others in your culture. Studies show that many middle- and upper-class students in North America, as well as Asian-American students, have internalized high expectations for achieving academic success. However, members of other cultures may not have the same beliefs to lift their motivation. See if you can spot a self-defeating generalization about a group to which you belong because of your race, religion, sex, economic class, age, ethnicity, ability, or geographical region. For example, a young woman in my writing class once told me she knew she was going to fail. It was only the first day of the class and I asked her why she thought that. "I'm from the country," she said, "and people from the country can't write." I asked where she had learned that. "My fifth-grade teacher told us," she replied. And her tone said, "There, that *proves* it."

Research shows that teacher expectations influence students' own expectations of academic success. Fortunately, many teachers hold very high expectations for their students. Sadly, some instructors hold low expectations for all students, while some hold low expectations just for students of a particular culture. If you've had such a teacher, or encounter one in college, don't allow a Victim mindset to buy into disempowering stereotypes such as people from the country can't write, or women can't learn math, or students with learning disabilities aren't college material, or older students have lost the ability to learn. Instead, employ a Creator mindset, set your own high expectations, and live up to them.

In a nutshell, the $V \times E = M$ formula says that your level of motivation in college is determined by multiplying your value score by your expectation score. For example, if the value you place on a college degree is high (say, a 10), but your expectation of success in college is low (say, a 1), then your motivation score will be very low (10). Similarly, if you put little value on a college degree (say a 2), even if your expectation for success in college is high (say, a 9), then once more, your motivation score will be very low (18). In either case, your low score suggests that you probably won't do what's required to succeed in college: to make goal-directed choices consistently, to give a high-quality effort regularly, and to persist despite inevitable obstacles and challenges. Sadly, then, you'll join the multitude of students who exit college long before earning a degree.

Probably you see where all of this leads. To stay motivated in college, first, you need ways to raise (or keep high) the **value** you place on college, including the academic degree you'll earn, the knowledge you'll gain, and the experiences you'll have while enrolled. Second, you need ways to raise (or keep high) the **expectation** you have of being successful in college while making what you consider to be a reasonable effort. With our exploration of effective reading skills in Chapter 2, we've already identified some important academic skills that, when mastered, will contribute to your high expectations for success in college. Throughout *On Course,* you'll encounter literally hundreds of other skills, both academic and otherwise, that can raise your realistic expectation of success in college even higher.

Students tend to internalize the beliefs teachers have about their ability and they rise and fall in achieving the level of expectation of their teachers.

Lynn Kell Spradlin

For now, however, we are going to focus on value. Only you can determine how much value a college education holds for you, but let's look at some of the benefits that others have attributed to achieving a degree beyond high school.

VALUE OF COLLEGE OUTCOMES

One of the most widely recognized benefits of a college degree is increased earning power. According to recent U.S. Census Bureau data, high school graduates earn an average of $1.2 million dollars during their working lives. However, if you complete a two-year associate's degree, that lifetime total goes up another $400,000. If you complete a four-year bachelor's degree, you can add another $500,000. That means college graduates earn nearly one million dollars more in their lifetimes than those who end their formal education with a high school degree. Think what that additional money could do to help you and the people you love live a good life.

Not only does a college degree offer increased earnings, it also opens doors to employment in many desirable professions. Six out of every 10 jobs now require some postsecondary education and training, according to data reported by the ERIC Clearinghouse on Higher Education. The U.S. Department of Labor reports that the number of jobs requiring advanced skills now grows at twice the rate of those requiring only basic skills.

A college degree confers many additional benefits. According to the Institute for Higher Education Policy and the Carnegie Foundation, college graduates enjoy . . .

- higher savings levels.
- improved working conditions.
- increased personal and professional mobility.
- improved health and life expectancy.
- improved quality of life for offspring.
- better consumer decision making.
- increased personal status.
- more hobbies and leisure activities.

College grads also become more open-minded, more cultured, more rational, more consistent, and less authoritarian. As a bonus, these benefits are passed on to their children.

Additionally, attaining a college degree can bring personal satisfaction and accomplishment. I once had a 76-year-old student who inspired our class with her determination "to finally earn the college degree that I cheated myself out of more than 50 years ago." Another valuable outcome of a college degree is the pride and esteem that many enjoy when they walk across the stage to receive their hard-earned diploma. And for some, a college degree is an essential step toward fulfilling a personal vision; such was true for my college roommate who, for as long as he could remember, dreamed of being a doctor (and today he is one).

> For learning to take place with any kind of efficiency students must be motivated. To be motivated, they must become interested. And they become interested when they are actively working on projects which they can relate to their values and goals in life.
>
> *Gus Tuberville, former president, William Penn College*

Table 3.1 One Student's Desired Outcomes

Desired Outcomes	Value
Earn a grade point average (GPA) of 3.8 or better and make the dean's list this semester.	A high GPA will look great on my transcript when I apply for a job. Also, it will give me a real boost of self-confidence.
In my English class, write at least one essay that contains no more than two nonstandard grammar errors.	I want to be able to write without worrying that someone who reads my work is going to think I'm stupid or illiterate.
In my Student Success class, learn at least three strategies for managing my time more effectively.	I feel overwhelmed and stressed with all I need to do, and learning how to manage my time better will lower my stress level.
Get an A in my accounting class.	I want a career in accounting, so doing well in this course is the first step toward success in my profession.
Make three or more new friends.	My friends from high school all went to other colleges or they're working. I want to make new friends here so I'll have people to hang out with on the weekends.

For some people, long-term goals are too distant to be motivating. They do get fired up, however, by short-term goals they can nearly touch, such as outcomes they can create during this semester. Table 3.1 shows the short-term goals that one of my students chose for himself, along with his reasons why.

VALUE OF COLLEGE EXPERIENCES

Value isn't found only in outcomes; it's also found in experiences. In fact, all human beings manage their emotions by doing their best to maximize positive experiences and minimize negative ones. What, for example, is the value of playing an intramural sport, attending a movie, belonging to a fraternity or sorority, dancing, playing a video game, or hanging out with friends? Primarily, all are choices to manage our inner experiences. If done in excess, any one of these choices can get us off course from our desired outcomes. But done in moderation, all of these activities (and many others) can create a positive experience and contribute greatly to academic motivation. That's because if you're enjoying the journey called college, you're much more likely to persist until you reach the destination called graduation.

So, what are your desired experiences in college? If someday in the future you were to tell someone that college was one of the best experiences of your life, what specifically would you have experienced? Many will say "fun." Fair enough. Then make fun happen. Your challenge is to experience fun while staying on course to academic success. And you can do it! Consider these options for fun: Join a club, play a sport, get to know a classmate, attend a party, learn

> Setting specific goals helps learners in at least three ways: The goals focus attention on important aspects of the task; they help motivate and sustain task mastery efforts; and they serve an information function by arming learners with criteria that they can use to assess and if necessary adjust their strategies as they work.
>
> *Jere Brophy*

something new that really interests you. Here are other experiences that my students desired: respect, relaxation, connection, self-confidence, an open mind, quiet reflection, passion for learning, total engagement, full-out participation, inspiration, challenge, courage, spirit of the group, self-acceptance, joy, pride, freedom, and an "Aha."

One of the students in my college success class said he wanted to experience "creativity." As an alternative to the final project, he proposed to write a rap song about the success principles he'd learned in our class. I told him he had my permission as long as he agreed to "rap" his project to our class on the last day of the semester. Little did I know that he was a professional rapper with a couple of CDs to his credit. As promised, he (and his whole group) showed up on the last day of the semester, handed out the words to "The College Success Rap," and treated us all to a rousing course finale. Best of all, he did a great job of demonstrating that he had learned many of the key principles of success, helping his classmates learn them even more deeply. Afterward he said, "Man, that was great!"

Table 3.2 lists the desired experiences that another of my students identified for herself, along with her reasons why.

German philosopher Friedrich Nietzsche once said, "He who has a *why* to live for can endure almost any *how*." He affirms that few obstacles can stop us when we understand the personal value we place on the outcomes and experiences of our journey. Discover your own motivation and your chances for success soar!

> What ultimately counts most for each person is what happens in consciousness: the moments of joy, the times of despair added up through the years determine what life will be like. If we don't gain control over the contents of consciousness we can't live a fulfilling life.
>
> *Mihaly Csikszentmihaly*

> He who puts in four hours of "want to" will almost always outperform the person who puts in eight hours of "have to."
>
> *Roger von Oech*

Table 3.2 One Student's Desired Experiences

Desired Experiences	Value
Fun	My brother dropped out of college because he said it was all work and no play. I know I'm going to have to work hard in college, but I want to have fun, too. I think if I'm enjoying myself, that'll make all the assignments more bearable.
Academic confidence	I've never done particularly well in school, although my teachers have always said I could be a good student if I applied myself more. I want to feel just as smart as any other student in my classes.
Excitement about learning	I didn't really like my classes in high school. I want to get excited about learning in at least one course, so I look forward to the homework and sometimes the class time goes so fast I can't believe when it's over.
Personal confidence	I have always been a shy person, and I want to become more outgoing so I can do well on future job interviews and be more assertive in my career so I get the promotions I deserve.

Designing a Compelling Life Plan

 **Focus Questions** If your life were as good as it could possibly be, what would it look like? What would you have, do, and be?

> Your goals are the road maps that guide you and show you what is possible for your life.
>
> Les Brown

While growing up, Joan dreamed of becoming a famous singer. Following high school, she started performing in night clubs. She married her manager, and the two of them lived in a motor home, driving from town to town in pursuit of singing jobs. After exhausting years on the road, Joan recorded a song. It didn't sell, and her dream began to unravel. Marital problems complicated her career. Career problems complicated her marriage. Joan grew tired of the financial and emotional uncertainty in her life. Finally, in frustration, she divorced her husband and gave up her dream of singing professionally.

Although disappointed, Joan started setting new goals. She needed to earn a living, so she set a short-term goal to become a hairdresser. After graduating from cosmetology school, Joan saved enough money to settle some debts, buy a car, and pay for a new long-term goal. She decided to go to a community college (where I met her) and major in dental hygiene.

Two years later, Joan graduated with honors and went to work in a dentist's office. Lacking a dream that excited her, Joan chose another long-term goal: earning her bachelor's degree. Joan worked days in the dentist's office and at night she attended classes. After a few years, she again graduated with honors.

Then, she set another long-term goal: earning her master's degree. Earlier in her life, Joan had doubted that she was "college material." With each academic success, her confidence grew. "One day I realized that once I set a goal, it's a done deal," Joan said.

This awareness inspired her to begin dreaming again. As a child, Joan had always imagined herself as a teacher, but her doubts had always steered her in other directions. Master's degree now in hand, she returned to our college to teach dental hygiene. A year later, she was appointed department chairperson. In only seven years, Joan had gone from a self-doubting first-year student to head of our college's dental hygiene department. Despite obstacles and setbacks, she continued to move in a positive direction, ever motivated by the promise of achieving personally valuable goals and dreams.

ROLES AND GOALS

According to psychologist Brian Tracy, many people resist setting life goals because they don't know how. Let's eliminate this barrier so you, like Joan, can experience the heightened motivation that accompanies personally meaningful goals.

First, think about the roles you have chosen for your life. A life role is an activity to which we regularly devote large amounts of time and energy. For example, you're presently playing the role of college student. How many of the following roles are you also playing: friend, employee, employer, athlete, brother, sister, church member, son, daughter, roommate, husband, wife, partner, parent, grandparent, tutor, musician, neighbor, volunteer? Do you play other roles as well? Most people identify four to seven major life roles. If you have more than seven, you may be spreading yourself too thin. Consider combining or eliminating one or more of your roles while in college. If you have identified fewer than four roles, assess your life again. You may have overlooked a role or two.

> The most important thing about motivation is goal setting. You should always have a goal.
>
> *Francie Larrieu Smith*

CATHY by Cathy Guisewite

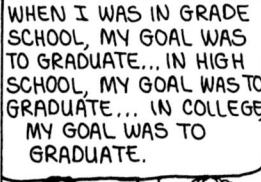

Once you identify your life roles, think about your long-term goals for each one. Identify what you hope to accomplish in this role in the next 2 to 5 or even 10 years. For example, in your role as a student, 10 years from now will you have a 2-year associate of arts (A.A.) degree? A four-year bachelor of arts (B.A.) or bachelor of science (B.S.) degree? Will you have attended graduate school to earn a master of arts (M.A.) or master of science (M.S.) degree? Or gone even farther to obtain a doctor of philosophy (Ph.D.) degree, a medical doctor (M.D.) degree, or a doctor of jurisprudence (J.D.) law degree? Any of these future academic goals could be yours.

HOW TO SET A GOAL

To be truly motivating, a goal needs five qualities. You can remember them by applying the DAPPS rule. "DAPPS" is an acronym, a memory device in which each letter of the word stands for one of five qualities: Dated, Achievable, Personal, Positive, and Specific.

Dated

Motivating goals have specific deadlines. A short-term goal usually has a deadline within a few months (like your semester's desired outcomes set in Journal Entry 9). A long-term goal generally has a deadline as far in the future as 1 year, 5 years, even 10 years (such as the goal you have for your most advanced academic degree). As your target deadline approaches, your motivation typically increases. This positive energy helps you finish strong. If you don't meet your deadline, you have an opportunity to examine what went wrong and create a new plan. Without a deadline, you might stretch the pursuit of a goal over your whole life, never reaching it.

Achievable

Motivating goals are challenging but realistic. It's unrealistic to say you'll run a marathon (26+ miles) next week if your idea of a monster workout has been opening and closing the refrigerator. Still, if you're going to err, err on the side of optimism. When you set goals at the outer reaches of your present ability, stretching to reach them causes you to grow. Listen to other people's advice, but trust yourself to know what is achievable for you. Apply this guideline: "Is achieving this goal at least 50 percent believable to me?" If so and you *really* value it, go for it!

Personal

Motivating goals are your own. They aren't thrust upon you by someone else. Be aware of pressure to conform to the expectations of others. Maybe you have a passion for graphic design but your parents want you to major in business so you can join the family business. Also be aware of subtle pressure to conform to the norms of your culture at the expense of what you want. For example, all cultures create expectations about what men and women *should*

One day Alice came to a fork in the road and saw a Cheshire cat in a tree. "Which road do I take?" she asked. "Where do you want to go?" was his response. "I don't know," Alice answered. "Then," said the cat, "it doesn't matter."

Lewis Carroll

Goals are dreams with a deadline.

Napoleon Hill

do, and, interestingly, gender-role stereotypes are similar across cultures. If you're a woman who wants to be an engineer, don't set a goal to be a dental hygienist. If you're a man who wants to be a kindergarten teacher, don't set a goal to be a lawyer. You don't want to be on your deathbed some day and realize you have lived someone else's life. Trust that you know better than anyone else what you want.

Positive

Motivating goals focus your energy on what you *do* want rather than on what you *don't* want. So translate negative goals into positive goals. For example, a negative goal not to fail a class becomes a positive goal to earn a grade of B or better. I recall a race car driver explaining how he miraculously kept his spinning car from smashing into the concrete racetrack wall: "I kept my eye on the track, not the wall." Likewise, focus your thoughts and actions on where you *do* want to go rather than where you *don't* want to go, and you, too, will stay on course.

> I always wanted to be somebody, but now I realize I should have been more specific.
>
> *Lily Tomlin*

Specific

Motivating goals state outcomes in specific, measurable terms. It's not enough to say, "My goal is to do better this semester" or "My goal is to work harder at my job." How will you know if you've achieved these goals? What specific, measurable evidence will you have? Revised, these goals become, "I will complete every college assignment this semester to the best of my ability" and "I will volunteer for all offerings of overtime at work." Being specific keeps you from fooling yourself into believing you've achieved a goal when, in fact, you haven't. It also helps you make choices that create positive results.

Through the years, I've had the joy of working with students who have had wonderful and motivating long-term goals: becoming an operating room nurse, writing and publishing a novel, traveling around the world, operating a refuge for homeless children, marrying and raising a beautiful family, playing professional baseball, starting a private school, composing songs for Aretha Franklin, becoming a college professor, swimming in the Olympics, managing an international mutual fund, having a one-woman art show, becoming a fashion model, getting elected state senator, owning a clothing boutique, and more. How about you? What do you *really* want?

> The future belongs to those who believe in the beauty of their dreams.
>
> *Eleanor Roosevelt*

DISCOVER YOUR DREAMS

Perhaps even more than goals do, dreams fuel our inner fire. They give our lives purpose and guide our choices. They provide motivating energy when we run headlong into an obstacle. When Candy Lightner's daughter was killed by a drunk driver, she transformed this tragedy into her dream to stop drunk driving, and her dream became the international organization Mothers Against Drunk Driving (MADD). I found my dream only after 20 years of college teaching: My passion is empowering students with the beliefs and behaviors essential for living

a rich and personally fulfilling life. Although it's difficult to define a dream, they're grand in size and fueled by strong emotions. Unlike goals, which usually fit into one of our life roles, dreams often take over our lives, inspire other people, and take on a life of their own. That's why I sometimes wonder if people have dreams or if dreams have people.

If you presently have a big dream, you know how motivating it is. If you don't have a big dream, you're certainly in the majority. Most people have not found a guiding dream, yet they can still have great lives. College, though, offers a wonderful opportunity to discover or expand your dreams. You'll be exposed to hundreds, even thousands, of new people, ideas, and experiences. With each encounter, be aware of your energy. If you feel your voltage rise, pay attention. Something within you is getting inspired. If you're fortunate enough to find such a dream, consider the pithy advice of philosopher Joseph Campbell: "Follow your bliss."

YOUR LIFE PLAN

Wise travelers use maps to locate their destination and identify the best route to get there. Similarly, Creators identify their goals and dreams and the most direct path there. In creating such a life plan, it helps to start with your destination in mind and work backwards. If you have a dream, accomplishing it becomes your ultimate destination. Or maybe your destination is the accomplishment of one or more long-term goals for your life roles. Because you can't complete a long journey in one step, your short-term goals become steppingstones, and each one completed brings you closer to the achievement of a long-term goal or dream.

Take a look at a page of a life plan that one student, Pilar, designed for herself. Although Pilar recorded her dream, not everyone will be able to do that. Her full life plan includes a page for each life role that she identified for herself, all of them with the same dream. Obviously, some life roles are going to make a more significant contribution to her dream than others. Notice that each long- and short-term goal adheres to the DAPPS rule.

> What is significant about a life plan is that it can help us live our own lives (not someone else's) as well as possible.
>
> Harriet Goldhor Lerner

MY DREAM: *I help families adopt older children (10 years old or older) and create home environments in which the children feel loved and supported to grow into healthy, productive adults.*

MY LIFE ROLE: *College student*

MY LONG-TERM GOALS IN THIS ROLE:

1. *I earn an associate of arts (A.A.) degree by June 2016.*
2. *I earn a bachelor of arts (B.A.) degree by June 2018.*
3. *I earn a master of social work (M.S.W.) degree by June 2020.*

MY SHORT-TERM GOALS IN THIS ROLE: *(this semester)*

1. *I achieve an A in English 101 by December 18.*
2. *I write a research paper on the challenges of adopting older children by November 20.*
3. *I achieve an A in Psychology 101 by December 18.*
4. *I learn and apply five or more psychological strategies that will help my family be happier and more loving by November 30.*
5. *I achieve an A in College Success by December 18.*
6. *I dive deep in every* On Course *journal entry, writing a minimum of 500 words for each one.*
7. *I learn five or more new success strategies and teach them to my younger brothers by November 30.*
8. *I take at least one page of notes in every class I attend this semester.*
9. *I turn in every assignment on time this semester.*
10. *I learn to use a computer well enough to prepare all of my written assignments by October 15.*

This is the first page of Pilar's six-page life plan. She wrote a similar page for each of her other five life roles: sister, daughter, friend, athlete, and employee at a group home for children.

Consciously designing your life plan, as Pilar did, has many benefits. A life plan defines your desired destinations in life and charts your best route for getting there. It gives your Inner Guide something positive to focus on when the chatter of your Inner Critic or Inner Defender attempts to distract you. And, like all maps, a life plan helps you get back on course if you get lost.

Perhaps most of all, a life plan is your personal definition of a life worth living. With it in mind, you'll be less dependent on someone else to motivate you. Your most compelling motivation will be found within.

> We... believe that one reason so many high-school and college students have so much trouble focusing on their studies is because they don't have a goal, don't know what all this studying is leading to.
>
> *Muriel James & Dorothy Jongeward*

> Many people fail in life, not for lack of ability or brains or even courage but simply because they have never organized their energies around a goal.
>
> *Elbert Hubbard*

 **Journal Entry 10**

In this activity, you will design one or more parts of your life plan. To focus your thoughts, glance back at Pilar's life plan and use it as a model.

1. **Title a new page in your journal: MY LIFE PLAN. Below the title, complete the part of your life plan for your role as a student.**

   My Dream: [If you have a compelling dream, describe it here. If you're not sure what your dream is, you can simply write, "I'm searching."]

   My Life Role: Student

Wise Choices in College

TAKING NOTES

In Chapter 2, we discussed the many hours you will spend in college **Collecting** information and skills from your reading assignments. In this chapter, we will examine the second most time-consuming way you will **Collect** information while in college: attending classes. In the pursuit of a four-year degree, students spend nearly 400 hours in a formal classroom. Students pursuing a two-year degree spend about half that time in class.

Your instructors, of course, expect you to learn what they cover in these class sessions. Unless you're motivated to take effective notes, however, most of what you hear in class will zip through your short-term memory and be quickly forgotten. More than one hundred years ago, Hermann Ebbinghaus conducted the first studies of memory and discovered that we lose about 75 percent of what we learn within twenty-four hours. That's why effective note-taking is an essential skill for achieving academic success in college.

Taking notes while attending a class is similar to taking notes while reading a textbook. However, taking notes during a class offers additional challenges. For one thing, as you mark or annotate a textbook, you stop reading. Thus, while reading you are in total control of how fast you receive new information. By contrast, when you take notes during a class, the speaker keeps talking. You have little or no control over the speed of information delivery. This situation places greater demands on your ability to identify key concepts, main ideas, and supporting details and write them down accurately and completely.

And that's not all. You're likely to encounter instructors who will provide their own unique obstacles to note-taking: They may speed talk until your head spins. Or . . . drone . . . on . . . so . . . sloooowly . . . you . . . have . . . trouble . . . staying . . . awake. They may be poorly organized. Or have accents that you have difficulty understanding. Some instructors may wander maddeningly from the topic or distract you with irritating mannerisms. Or all of the above.

A summary of research on note-taking compiled by Kenneth Kiewra reports sobering news. Lecture notes taken by first-year students contain, on average, only 11 percent of the critical ideas presented during a class. No matter how well you study, you can't pass tests if you are studying only 11 percent of the important ideas in a course.

You can choose to complain, blame, and make excuses for why it's impossible to take good notes in a class. Or, you can take full responsibility for your learning outcomes and experiences. Regardless of how many obstacles the instructor or the subject presents, it's your job to take effective notes. In this chapter you'll learn how.

TAKING NOTES: THE BIG PICTURE

To take effective class notes, you need to answer two key questions: *What* should I write in my notes and *how* should I write that information?

First, consider what to write in your notes. Despite a popular misconception, the answer is not "everything the instructor says." Even if you could write that fast, having a word-for-word transcript of a class is not the goal of note-taking. As with reading, the goal of note-taking is **Collecting** key concepts, main ideas, and supporting details. Thus, much of what you learned earlier about taking notes while reading also applies to taking notes in class. But you'll need some new strategies to compensate for the challenges of writing notes while someone is speaking.

As for how to write your notes, a number of note-taking systems have been invented, but essentially they all fit into one of two categories: linear or graphic. Examples of these methods will be explained in this chapter.

Many students worry about taking perfect class notes because they use their notes to study for tests. In the CORE Learning System, however, you do not study from either your class notes or your textbooks. Instead, as you'll learn in the next chapter, after **Collecting** key concepts, main ideas, and supporting details from all sources, you'll **Organize** this information into effective study materials. It is these materials that will help you create deep and lasting learning. For now, simply examine the note-taking strategies that follow and choose the ones that you think will best help you **Collect** important knowledge during each class. No single method of note-taking works best for everyone, so experiment and personalize a note-taking system that works best for you.

As you examine the following strategies, keep in mind that the big picture of note-taking is essentially the same as for reading: **You are Collecting key concepts, main ideas, and supporting details.**

BEFORE TAKING NOTES

1. Create a positive affirmation about taking notes. Some students hold negative beliefs about their ability to take good notes or the value of doing so. Create an affirming statement about taking notes. For example, *I take notes that record all of the main ideas and supporting details, making learning easy and fun.* Along with your personal affirmation, repeat this note-taking affirmation to motivate new learning attitudes and behaviors.

2. Assemble appropriate supplies. Experiment and decide on the best note-taking supplies for you. Find a pen you like writing with. Keep your notes in ring binders, composition books, spiral binders, or a laptop computer. Ring binders are handy because you can add and remove pages easily. This option is helpful when an instructor provides handouts or you revise your notes. If you use one binder for all of your classes, use tabs to separate the notes for each class. If you take class notes on a laptop computer, be sure to back up your files often to avoid the disaster of losing notes because of a hard-drive crash.

3. Complete homework assignments before class. Remember, neural networks created by prior learning make new learning easier. That's why completing assignments before class increases your ability to understand lectures and discussions. Also, you'll know what belongs in your notes. For example, you'll know if the instructor is repeating what was in the reading or adding new information. And, suppose the instructor's presentation style presents a challenge (such as speed talking). Because the information is already familiar, you'll more easily spot key concepts, main ideas, and supporting details. If your homework includes solving problems, complete them before class as well.

4. Prepare a list of questions. After completing homework assignments, write questions you have about the information. If you write them on binder paper, leave a space after each question for the answer. If you write questions on 3" × 5" cards, you can put answers on the other side. If you place questions in a computer file, it's easy to type in the answers. Bring these questions to class, study group meetings, tutoring sessions, or a conference with your instructor.

5. Attend every class. As obvious as this suggestion may seem, some students don't create good notes simply because they aren't in class. Sure, you can borrow notes from another student. But is it smart to bet your academic success on another student's note-taking skill? Remember, research reveals that first-year students' notes contain only 11 percent of the important ideas presented during a class. Your notes, after applying the strategies in this chapter, will be far more effective than that!

6. Be organized. At the end of each term, you'll have note pages galore for each course. To keep them organized, write some or all of the following information at the top of each note page:

- Course name
- Date of the class
- Topic of the class (usually listed in the course syllabus)
- Any associated reading assignments (also usually listed in the course syllabus)
- Page number (in case your notes get mixed up later)

WHILE TAKING NOTES

First, let's consider WHAT to write in your notes.

7. Listen actively for key concepts, main ideas, and supporting details. <u>C</u>ollecting this information *accurately* and *completely* takes active listening. When you listen actively, you're able to reflect back what a speaker says. In a conversation with a friend, you might reflect: *Sounds like you had an exciting time white water rafting last weekend.* Or in a music class, you might reflect, *So, you're saying a divertimento is a short musical piece that was popular during the Classical period.* When taking notes, you'd simply write an abbreviated version of this reflection: *Divertimento—a short musical piece popular during the Classical period.* Be aware that inner chatter competes with active listening, so quiet your Inner Critic and Inner Defender during class. Don't judge yourself: *I have no clue what she's talking about; I am such a dunce.* And don't judge others: *This jerk is the worst teacher on the planet.* Replace judgments with an active effort to hear all of the speaker's key concepts, main ideas, and supporting details. After all, if you don't <u>C</u>ollect the course information completely and accurately, then your entire learning effort is sabotaged from the start. See pages 158–159 for more suggestions to improve active listening.

8. Ask and answer questions. When you bring questions to class, raise your hand and ask. When your instructor asks a question, raise your hand and answer. When you don't understand an idea, raise your hand and ask: *Excuse me, Professor, what holds atoms together in a molecule?* Or, if you're too confused to formulate a question, simply request more information: *Would you please say more about Kant's idea that metaphysics can be reformed through epistemology?* If asking a question isn't an option, leave a space in your notes and write a question in the margin. Many options exist for later filling in the answer: Listen for the instructor to answer your question during the class. Visit the instructor during his or her office hours. Look for the missing information in your textbook. Ask a classmate or study group member for help. Seek assistance at your college's tutoring center.

9. Listen for verbal cues. Instructors will often provide verbal cues to introduce a main idea or supporting detail, thus helping you decide *what* to write in your notes. When you hear any of the following, get ready to record an important idea: *The point is . . . The following is very important . . . Be sure to write this next idea in your notes . . . On page 135 underline the following . . . Let me repeat that . . . The key here is . . . That's a great answer to my question . . . A third component is . . . The main symptom of this problem is . . . The next step for solving this problem is . . . If you remember only one thing from today's class, remember that . . . The key point here is . . .* (and the granddaddy of them all) *This will be on the test.* Also, instructors often give verbal cues before presenting supporting details. When you hear any of the following, get ready to record one or more supporting details: *To illustrate this point . . . Evidence for this includes . . . A good example is . . . To explain that idea further . . . This was proven in a study that showed . . .* Listen for additional kinds of supporting details such as personal experiences, experiments, dates, anecdotes, definitions, lists, names, facts, and data.

Now, we'll consider HOW to write your notes.

10. Take notes with an outline. Now that we've looked at ways to determine *what* to put in your notes, let's consider the second critical choice: *how* to write your notes. As mentioned earlier, the two general methods of note-taking are linear and graphic. First, we'll consider linear notes, which are the more common of the two. When you take notes in a linear fashion, you record ideas as much as possible in the order they are presented ("linear" means in a line). Outlines are good for this. They record ideas and supporting details on separate lines, using indentations to indicate levels of importance. You can view an example of an informal outline in Figure 3.1. Note the use of short phrases instead of full sentences to greatly condense what the speaker says. Here's how to take notes with an outline:

- Write a *key concept* at the top of a page. This information is usually expressed in a word or phrase. This might be the title of a chapter or a key word in the instructor's course outline. For example, the key concept in a history class might be "Causes of World War II," in a biology class it might be "Cell Communication," and in a psychology class it could be "Abraham Maslow."
- Record *main ideas (level 1)* beginning at the left margin. For a formal outline, start each level 1 line with a Roman numeral (e.g., I, II, III, IV).
- Under each main idea, indent a few spaces and record related *secondary ideas (level 2)*. For a formal outline, start each level 2 line with a capital letter (e.g., A, B, C, D).
- Under each secondary idea, indent a few more spaces and record any related *major supporting details (level 3)*. For a formal outline, begin each level 3 line with an Arabic numeral (e.g., 1, 2, 3, 4).
- If you need to add *minor supporting details (level 4)*, indent those lines a few more spaces and, for a formal outline, begin those lines with small letters (e.g., a, b, c, d).

Outlines are most helpful when instructors present well-organized lectures. If your instructor provides printed lecture notes or uses PowerPoint slides, you've probably got an organized instructor. If, however, your instructor jumps from topic to topic and back again, all is not lost. That's when a concept map can ride to the rescue.

11. Take notes with a concept map. In this graphic note-taking method, *where* you place information (key concepts, main ideas, and supporting details) on the page shows both their level of importance and their relationship to one another. In general, ideas placed closer to the middle are more important than ideas placed farther away from the middle. Figure 3.2 shows an example of a concept map with content. Here's how to take notes with a concept map:

- Write the *key concept* in the middle of a page; then underline or draw a circle around it. This information is usually just a word or phrase. For example, if the topic of a class session is "Photosynthesis" or "Logical Fallacies" or "Abraham Maslow," that is what you would write in the middle of the page.
- Write *main ideas (level 1)* near the key concept, underline or circle them, and draw lines connecting them to the key concept.
- Write *secondary ideas (level 2)* near their related main idea, underline or circle them, and draw lines connecting them to the related main ideas.
- Write *major supporting details (level 3)* near their related secondary idea, underline or circle them, and draw lines connecting them to the related secondary idea.
- Write *minor supporting details (level 4)* near their related major supporting idea, underline or circle them, and draw lines connecting them to the related major supporting idea.

Concept maps are helpful when lecturers leap from idea to idea. They are also good for taking notes

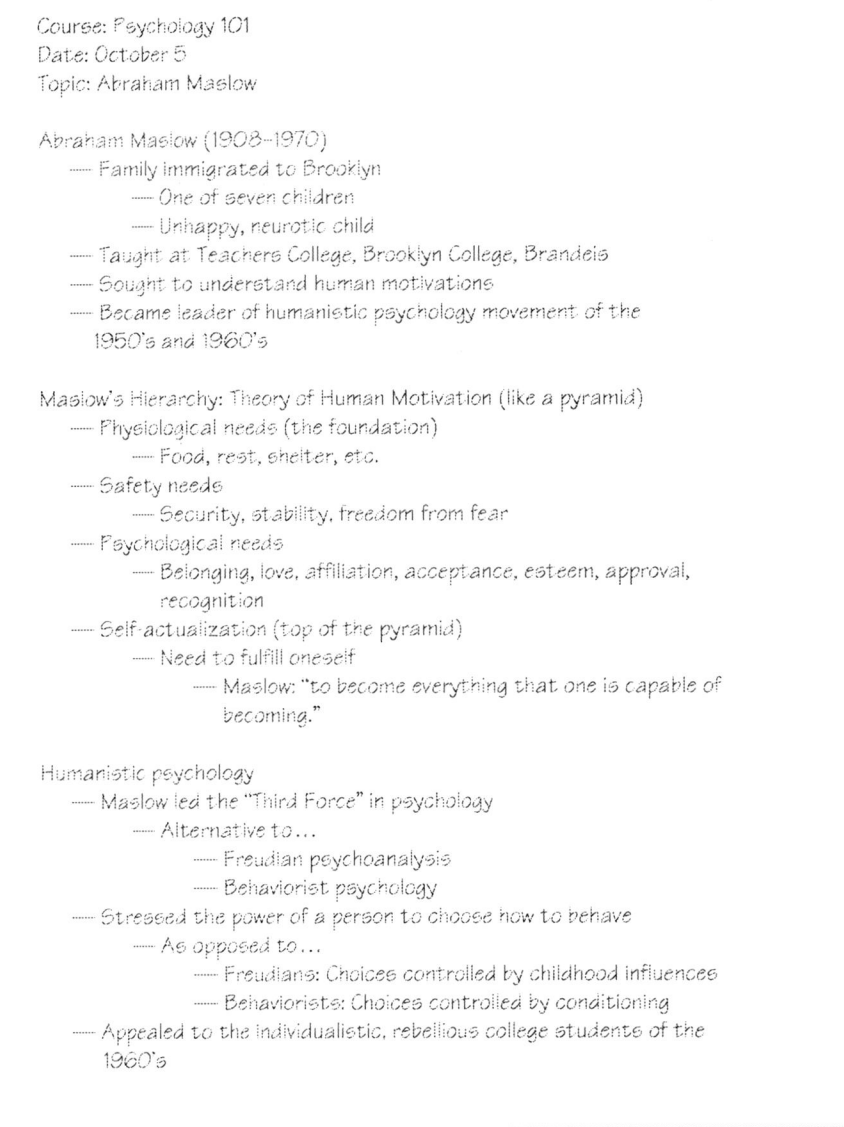

Figure 3.1 Informal Outline Example
Source: From Carol Kanar, *The Confident Student*, Third Edition, p. 353. Copyright © 1998 by Houghton Mifflin Company. Used by permission.

on class discussions that move back and forth between topics. As a speaker returns to an earlier idea, go to that part of the concept map, add the new information, circle or underline it, and draw a line connecting it to related information. The visual nature of a concept map makes it especially appealing to students who like a picture of what they are learning.

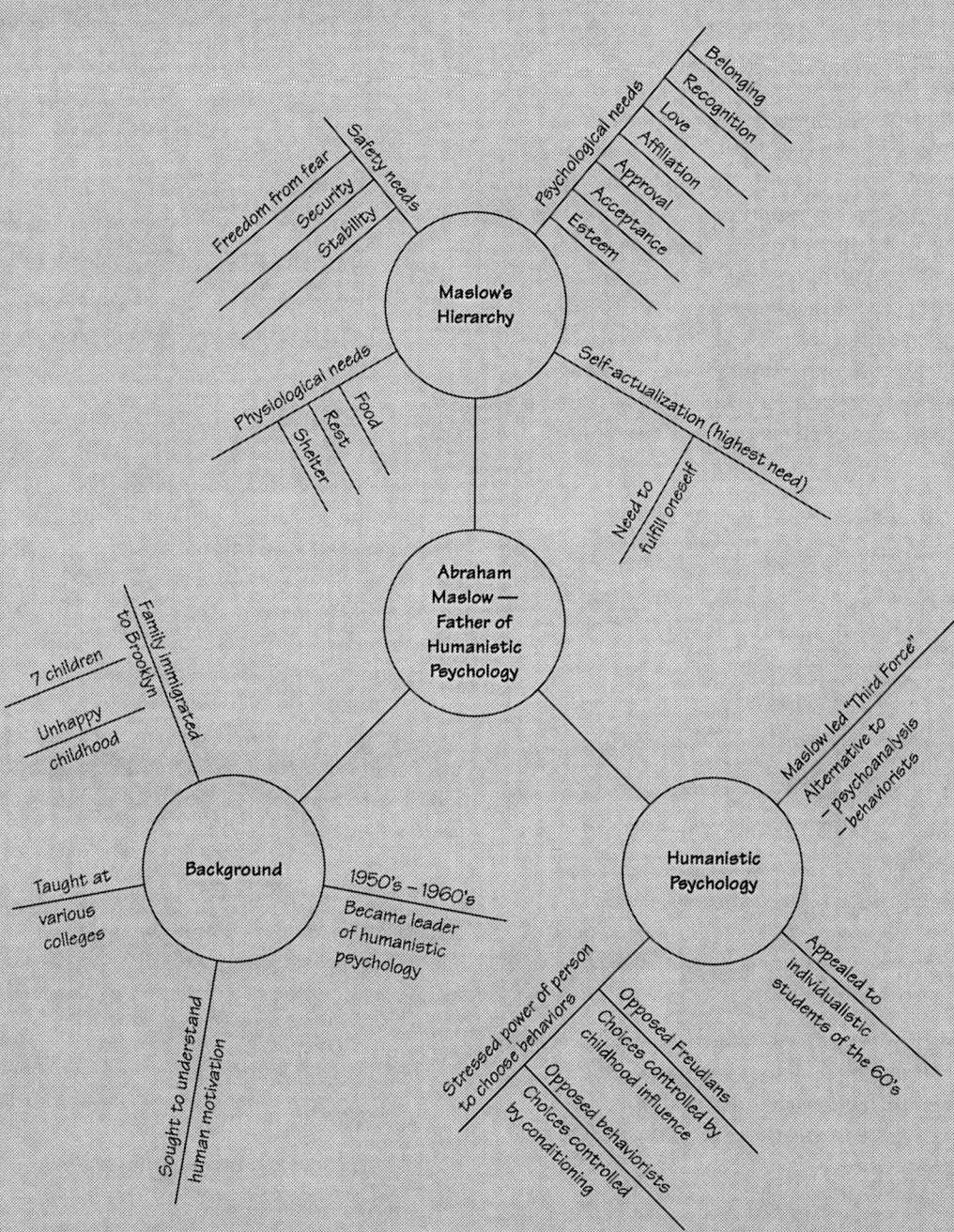

Figure 3.2 Concept Map Example

12. Use three-column notes for mathematics. Since math instructors spend much class time demonstrating how to solve problems, a three-column approach is extremely helpful for **Collecting** their methods. First, divide your note page into three columns. Title the left-hand column "Problem," the middle column "Solution," and the right-hand column "Explanation." When the instructor presents a problem, write it in the left column. As the instructor demonstrates how to solve the problem, write all steps in the middle column, making sure you understand each one. In the right-hand column, add any explanation that will help you understand how to solve similar problems. For example, you might add an explanation of each step or convert unfamiliar symbols into words.

Structure of Three-Column Math Notes

Problem	Solution	Explanation
The math problem as presented by the instructor	Step 1 Step 2 Step 3 Step 4 Step 5 Etc.	Elaboration to explain steps of the solution

You'll find an example of three-column math notes on page 145.

13. Speed up note-taking. Most speakers talk much faster than you can write (or even type, if using a computer), so here are three strategies for speeding up your note-taking:

- *Condense*: Instead of attempting to write everything, listen for a couple of minutes, identify the key concept, a main idea, and one or two secondary ideas, and then paraphrase them in your own words.

- *Leave a blank space*: When you miss something, skip down a few lines, and pick up writing what is being said now. As with unanswered questions, you can return later to fill in the blank space in a number of ways: ask the instructor (in class, if appropriate, or during office hours), ask a classmate, ask a tutor, or review your reading assignment for the missing information.

- *Use abbreviations*: Create your own personal shorthand. The following are some possible abbreviations:

Ex	example	&	and
con't	continued	dept	department
imp	important	→	leads to
#	number	=	equals
1st	first	vs	versus
w/	with	w/o	without
nec	necessary	etc	and other things

14. Record the class. If you try the previous suggestions and still aren't happy with the quality of your notes, ask your instructor for permission to record the class. You can listen to the recording as many times as needed to fill in gaps in your notes or review difficult concepts. *Caution*: Don't procrastinate until you have forty-five hours of recorded class sessions to listen to and only twenty-four hours before the final exam. Instead, listen often to short segments. Each time, practice different note-taking strategies until you perfect your own personalized system.

AFTER TAKING NOTES

15. Polish your notes within twenty-four hours. As soon as possible after each class, make sure your notes are *accurate*, *complete*, and *understandable*. Do some or all of the following:

- Finish partial sentences.
- Expand on key words.
- Fill in spaces with missing information.
- Correct misspellings.
- Clarify unreadable words and confusing sentences.
- Delete unnecessary information.

- Revise drawings or charts.
- Correct steps in problem solving.

Afterward, if you still have gaps or confusion in your notes, meet with classmates, a tutor, or your instructor to address the problems. Not only does this action provide you with polished notes, it continues the active process of creating deep and lasting learning.

16. Compare notes. Compare your notes with those of your study group members or other motivated classmates. See if others have **Collected** important information that you missed. See where their notes may have different information and decide whose version is more accurate. This effort will help you all **Collect** additional information and further polish your notes.

NOTE-TAKING EXERCISE

In an upcoming class, take notes in a new way. Compare your experimental notes with those of a classmate, seeing which of you has recorded more complete and accurate information for later studying.

A BIT OF HERESY

In many study skills books, another method of note-taking is usually presented. Named for the university where it originated, the Cornell Method calls for note paper to be divided into three sections (see page 146 for the structure). Section A is used for recording notes from a reading assignment or class session. However, the Cornell Method offers no unique suggestions about *how* to record notes in that section. Sections B and C are employed later for adding key words, questions, and summaries, so they also offer no guidance about *how* to take notes. Thus, although the Cornell Method is usually presented as a note-taking system, it actually offers no strategies for *how* to take notes while reading or attending class (only *where* to record them). So, in the CORE Learning System, the Cornell Method is not considered a note-taking method. It is, however, a very powerful method for **Rehearsing** and **Evaluating** learning, so we will examine the use of this valuable learning strategy in Chapter 4.

Creating a Support System

 **Focus Question** How could you make accomplishing your success a little easier and a lot more fun?

What part will others play in your quest to achieve your goals and dreams? And what part will you play in theirs?

How you answer these questions will affect your level of success in college and beyond. As with so many aspects of life, your culture has programmed you to make its approved choices. And there is probably no other area where cultures are more clearly different than in their beliefs about the role that people play in one another's lives.

At one end of this spectrum are **individualistic** cultures. These cultures have an "I/me" orientation, and independence is highly regarded. At the other end of this spectrum are **collectivistic** cultures. These cultures have a "we/us" orientation and interdependence is highly regarded. Look back at the *On Course* Self-Assessment in Chapter 1 and note your score for "Employing Interdependence." If it was low, you likely have an individualistic mindset. If your score was high, you likely have a collectivistic mindset.

Mainstream North American culture has a strongly individualistic mindset, according to researcher Geert Hofstede. In this culture, rugged individualism and personal success are highly regarded, and each person is seen as a unique individual. When children reach adulthood, they are expected to strike out on their own and compete for success. Individualistic cultures admire people who "stand on their own two feet," who "pull themselves up by their boot straps," who "stand out in a crowd," and who are "self-made" men and women. Feeling good about oneself is related to one's personal accomplishments.

By contrast, other cultures—Latino, Asian, and Native American cultures among them—have a collectivistic mindset. These cultures value social harmony and family honor. They respect those who fit in and enhance the welfare of the group. Whereas individualistic cultures believe "the squeaky wheel gets the grease," collectivistic cultures believe "The goose that honks gets shot" or "The nail that sticks up gets pounded down." Family unity, honor, and respect are vital parts of collectivistic cultures. The importance of family is demonstrated by lifelong caring for both immediate and extended family members. Three or even four generations of family members may live near, or even with, one another. Feeling good about oneself is related to one's contribution to others, including family, workplace, and culture.

Each of these cultural perspectives has advantages and disadvantages. Creators, however, see beyond their cultural programming. They know there is a time to be independent and a time to be interdependent. With this perspective, they multiply the number of options they have at each new fork in the road. My experience is that most students choose independence far more

> Ask yourself: When making a choice, do you first and foremost consider what you want, what will make you happy, or do you consider what is best for you *and* the people around you? . . . Where we fall on this continuum is very much a product of our cultural upbringing and the script we are given for how to choose. . . .
>
> *Sheena Iyengar*

> Even as people take pride in their national independence, we know we are becoming more and more interdependent.
>
> *Bill Clinton*

often than interdependence. As a result, they can benefit from using more of the resources their colleges provide to help them succeed. Let's consider some choices you could make to create a support system that will help you not only achieve your goals in college but make the journey less stressful.

SEEK HELP FROM YOUR INSTRUCTORS

Building positive relationships with your college instructors is a powerful Quadrant II action that can pay off handsomely. Your instructors have years of specialized training. You've already paid for their help with your tuition, and all you have to do is ask.

Find out your professors' office hours and make an appointment. Arrive prepared with questions or requests, and you'll likely get good help. As a bonus, by getting to know your instructors, you may find a mentor who will help you in college and beyond.

GET HELP FROM COLLEGE RESOURCES

Nearly every college spends a chunk of tuition money to provide support services for students, but these services go to waste unless you use them. Do you know what support services your college offers, where they are, and how to use them?

Confused About Future Courses to Take?

Get help from your advisor or someone in the counseling center. They can help you decide on a major and create a multiyear academic plan that includes all of your required courses and their prerequisites.

Academic Problems?

Get help at one of your college's tutoring labs. Many colleges have a writing lab, a reading lab, and a math lab. Other sources of academic assistance might include a science learning center or a computer lab. Your college may also have a diagnostician who tests students for learning disabilities and suggests ways of overcoming them.

Money Problems?

Get help from your college's financial aid office. Money is available in grants and scholarships (which you don't pay back), loans (which you do pay back, usually at low interest rates), and student work programs (which offer jobs on campus). Your college may also have a service that can locate an off-campus job, perhaps one in the very career field you want to enter after graduation. In Chapter 8, you'll find detailed information about addressing your money problems (see pages 280–288).

> For every one of us that succeeds, it's because there's somebody there to show you the way out. The light doesn't always necessarily have to be in your family; for me it was teachers and school.
>
> Oprah Winfrey

Personal Problems?

Get help from your college's counseling office. Trained counselors are available at many colleges to help students through times of emotional upset. It's not unusual for students to experience some sort of personal difficulty during college; Creators seek assistance.

Health Problems?

Get aid from your college's health service. Many colleges have doctors who see students at little or no cost. Health-related products may be available inexpensively or even for free. Your college may even offer special health insurance for students.

Problems Deciding on a Career?

Get help from your college's career office. There you can take aptitude tests, discover job opportunities, learn to write or improve your résumé, and practice effective interviewing skills.

Problems Getting Involved Socially at Your College?

Request assistance from your college's student activities office. Here you'll discover athletic teams, trips, choirs, dances, service projects, student professional organizations, the college newspaper, the campus literary magazine, clubs, and more, just waiting for you to get involved.

CREATE A PROJECT TEAM

If you're tackling a big project, why not create a team to help? A project team is formed to accomplish one particular task. In business, when a project needs attention, an *ad hoc* committee is formed. *Ad hoc* in Latin means "toward this." In other words, an *ad hoc* committee comes together for the sole purpose of solving one problem. Once the task is complete, the committee disbands.

One of my students created a project team to help her move. More than a dozen classmates volunteered, including a fellow who provided a truck. In one Saturday morning, the team packed and delivered her possessions to a new apartment. Without the help of a team, how long would the move have taken her, how much would it have cost, and how much stress would it have caused her?

What big project do you have that would benefit from the assistance of others? The only barrier standing between you and a project team is your unwillingness to ask for help.

START A STUDY GROUP

In the late 1970s and early 1980s, a mathematics graduate student at the University of California, Berkeley, showed the value of academic study groups. Uri Treisman had noticed that students who succeeded in calculus met outside of class and, among other things, talked about solving math problems. Struggling

---

Alone we can do so little; together we can do so much.

Helen Keller

We are all interdependent. Do things for others—tribe, family, community—rather than just for yourself.

Chief Wilma Mankiller

My driving belief is this: great teamwork is the only way to reach our ultimate moments, to create the breakthroughs that define our careers, to fulfill our lives with a sense of lasting significance.

Pat Riley, former professional basketball coach

students didn't. As a result of this observation, Treisman created a program for struggling calculus students. His approach encouraged these students to gather for the purpose of talking about mathematics and solving challenging problems. The program was so successful that it has since been offered at many other colleges and universities. You can create a variation of Triesman's program in any course you want. Simply start a study group with some of your classmates. A study group differs from a project team in two ways. First, a study group is created to help everyone on the team excel in a particular course. Second, a study group meets many times throughout a semester. In fact, some study groups are so helpful that their members stay together throughout college.

Study groups offer a number of benefits. Participation increases your active involvement with the course content, which in turn leads to deeper learning and higher grades. The resulting academic success raises your expectations for success and increases your level of motivation. Study group participation helps you develop the skill of working with a group, a skill much sought after by employers. And some study group members may become your lifelong friends. Here are three suggestions for maximizing the value of your study group:

1. **CHOOSE ONLY CREATORS.** As the semester begins, make a list of potential study group members: classmates who attend regularly, come prepared, and participate actively. Also watch for that quiet student who doesn't say much but whose occasional comments reveal a special understanding of the subject. After the first test or essay, find out how the students on your list performed and invite three or four of the most successful to study with you.

2. **CHOOSE GROUP GOALS.** Regardless of potential, a study group is only as effective as you make it. Everyone should agree upon common goals. You might say to prospective study group members, "My goal in our math class is to master the subject and earn an A. Is that what you want, too?" Team up with students whose goals match or exceed your own.

3. **CHOOSE GROUP RULES.** The last step is establishing team rules. Pat Riley, one of the most successful professional basketball coaches ever, had his players create a "team covenant." Before the season, they agreed on the rules they would follow to stay on course to their goal of a championship. Your team should do the same. Decide where, how often, and at what time you'll meet. Most important, agree on what will happen during the meetings. Many study groups fail because they turn into social gatherings. Yours will succeed if you adopt rules like these:

   Rule 1: *We meet in the library every Thursday afternoon from one o'clock to three o'clock.*

   Rule 2: *All members bring their favorite study materials, including 20 new questions with answers and sources (e.g., textbook page or class notes).*

Love thy neighbor as thyself, but choose your neighborhood.

Louise Beal

If people around you aren't going anywhere, if their dreams are no bigger than hanging out on the corner, or if they're dragging you down, get rid of them. Negative people can sap your energy so fast, and they can take your dreams away from you, too.

Earvin (Magic) Johnson

> Until recently, the "old girls" did not know how the "old boys" network operated.... Women now know that, besides hard work and lots of skill, the move to the top requires a supportive network.
>
> June E. Gabler

Rule 3: *All study materials are discussed and all written questions are asked, answered, and understood before any socializing.*

One student I know took this advice and started a study group in his anatomy and physiology class, a course with a notoriously high failure rate. At the end of the semester, he proudly showed me a thank-you card signed by the other four members of his group. "We couldn't have done it without you," they wrote. "Thanks for *making* us get together!" Defying the odds, everyone in the group had passed the course.

Whom you spend time with will dramatically affect your outcomes and experiences in college. If you hang out with people who place little value on learning or a college degree, it's challenging to resist their negative influence. However, if you associate with highly committed, hard-working students, their encouragement can motivate you to stay on course to graduation even when the road gets rough. One of my students actually moved to a new apartment when he realized that "friends" from his old neighborhood spent most of their time putting down his efforts to get a college degree. When it comes to selecting your "group" in college, be sure to choose people who want out of life what you do.

Many people collaborate only with others who are like them. One of the greatest benefits of your college experience is meeting people of diverse backgrounds, with different cultures, beliefs, customs, ideas, skills, experiences, abilities, and resources. Be sure to network with those who are older or younger than you, who are from different states or countries, who are of different races or cultures, and who have different religions or political preferences. Exposure to such differences will expand your horizons and enhance your life.

Start a contact list of the people you meet in college. You might even want to write a few notes about them: their major or career field, names of family members, hobbies, interests, and especially their strengths. Keep in touch with these people during and after college.

Creators develop mutually supportive relationships in college that continue to support them for years—even for a lifetime. Don't get so bogged down with the daily demands of college that you fail to create an empowering support network.

BELIEVING IN YOURSELF

Be Assertive

 **Focus Question** How can you communicate in a style that strengthens relationships, creates better results, and builds strong self-esteem?

On rare occasions, we may encounter someone who doesn't want us to achieve our goals and dreams. Much more often, though, we run across folks who are too busy, too preoccupied, or couldn't care less about helping us. Meeting such people is especially likely in a bureaucracy such as a college or university. How we communicate our desires to them has a profound impact not only on the quality of the relationships and results we create, but on our self-esteem as well.

According to family therapist Virginia Satir, the two most common patterns of ineffective communication are **placating** and **blaming**. Both perpetuate low self-esteem.

- **PLACATING.** Victims who placate are dominated by their Inner Critic. They place themselves below others, protecting themselves from the sting of criticism and rejection by saying whatever they think will gain approval. Picture placators on their knees, looking up with a pained smile, nodding and agreeing on the outside, while fearfully hiding their true thoughts and feelings within. "*Please, please approve of me,*" they beg as their own Inner Critic judges them unworthy. To gain this approval, placators often spend time in Quadrant III doing what is urgent to others but unimportant to their own goals and dreams. Satir estimated that about 50 percent of people use placating as their major communication style.

- **BLAMING.** Victims who blame are dominated by their Inner Defender. They place themselves above others, protecting themselves from disappointment and failure by making others fully responsible for their problems. Picture them sneering down, a finger jabbing judgmentally at those below. Their Inner Defender snarls, "*You never . . . Why do you always . . . ? Why don't you ever . . . ? It's your fault that. . . .*" Satir estimated that about 30 percent of people use blaming as their major communication style.

Either passively placating or aggressively blaming keeps Victims from developing mutually supportive relationships, making the accomplishment of their dreams more difficult. The inner result is damaged self-esteem.

LEVELING

What, then, is the communication style of Creators? Some have called this style *assertiveness*: honestly expressing opinions and requests. Satir calls this

> Once a human being has arrived on this earth, communication is the largest single factor determining what kinds of relationships she or he makes with others and what happens to each in the world.
>
> *Virginia Satir*

> Learning to perceive the truth within ourselves and speak it clearly to others is a delicate skill, certainly as complex as multiplication or long division, but very little time is spent on it in school.
>
> *Gay & Kathlyn Hendricks*

communication style *leveling*. Leveling is characterized by a simple, yet profound, communication strategy: asserting the truth as you see it.

Creators boldly express their personal truth without false apology or excuse, without harsh criticism or blame. Leveling requires a strong Inner Guide and a commitment to honesty. Here are three strategies that promote leveling:

> I speak straight and do not wish to deceive or be deceived.
>
> *Cochise*

1. **COMMUNICATE PURPOSEFULLY.** Creators express a clear purpose even in times of emotional upset. If a Creator goes to a professor to discuss a disappointing grade, she will be clear whether her purpose is to (1) increase her understanding of the subject, (2) seek a higher grade, (3) criticize the instructor's grading ability, or accomplish some other option. By knowing her purpose, she has a way to evaluate the success of her communication. The Creator states purposefully, *When I saw my grade on this lab report, I was very disappointed. I'd like to go over it with you and learn how to improve my next one.*

2. **COMMUNICATE HONESTLY.** Creators candidly express unpopular thoughts and upset feelings in the service of building mutually supportive relationships. The Creator says honestly, *I'm angry that you didn't meet me in the library to study for the sociology test as you agreed.*

3. **COMMUNICATE RESPONSIBLY.** Because responsibility lies within, Creators express their personal responsibility with I-messages. An I-message allows creators to take full responsibility for their reaction to anything another person may have said or done. An effective I-message has four elements:

A statement of the situation:	*When you . . .*
A statement of your reaction:	*I felt/thought/decided . . .*
A request:	*I'd like to ask that you . . .*
An invitation to respond:	*Will you agree to that?*

> We should replace our alienating, criticizing words with "I" language. Instead of, "You are a liar and no one can trust you," say, "I don't like it when I can't rely on your words—it is difficult for us to do things together."
>
> *Ken Keyes*

Let's compare Victim and Creator responses to the same situation. Imagine that you feel sick one day and decide not to go to your history class. You phone a classmate, and she agrees to call you after class with what you missed. But she never calls. At the next history class, the instructor gives a test that was announced the day you were absent, and you fail it. Afterward, your classmate apologizes: "Sorry I didn't call. I was swamped with work." What response do you choose?

Placating: *Oh, don't worry about it. I know you had a lot on your mind. I probably would have failed the test anyway.*

Blaming: *You're the lousiest friend I've ever had! After making me fail that test, you have some nerve even talking to me!*

Leveling: *I'm angry that you didn't call. I realize that I could have called you, but I thought I could count on you to keep your word. If we're going to be friends, I need to know if you're going to keep your promises to me in the future. Will you?*

Notice that the leveling response is the only one of the three that positively addresses the issue, nurtures a relationship of equals, and demonstrates high self-esteem.

MAKING REQUESTS

Making effective requests is another demonstration of both assertiveness and high self-esteem. Creators know they can't reach their greatest goals and dreams alone, so they ask for help. The key to making effective requests is applying the DAPPS rule. Whenever possible, make your requests **D**ated, **A**chievable, **P**ersonal, **P**ositive, and (above all) **S**pecific. Here are some translations of vague Victim requests to specific, clear Creator requests:

Victim Requests	Creator Requests
1. I'm going to be absent next Friday. It sure would be nice if someone would let me know if I miss anything.	1. John, I'm going to be absent next Friday. Would you be willing to call me Friday night and tell me what I missed?
2. I don't suppose you'd consider giving me a few more days to complete this research paper?	2. I'd like to request an extension on my research paper. I promise to hand it in by noon on Thursday. Would that be acceptable?

When you make specific requests, the other person can respond with a clear "yes" or "no." If the person says "no," all is not lost. Try negotiating:

1. *If you can't call me Friday night, could I call you Saturday morning to find out what I missed?*
2. *If Thursday noon isn't acceptable to you, could I turn my paper in on Wednesday by 5:00?*

A Creator seeks definite yes or no answers. Victims often accept "maybe" or "I'll try" for fear of getting a "no," but it's better to hear a specific "no" and be free to move on to someone who will say "yes."

One of my mentors offered a valuable piece of advice: "If you go through a whole day without getting at least a couple of 'no's,' you aren't asking for enough help in your life."

SAYING "NO"

Saying "no" is another tool of the assertive Creator. When I think of the power of saying "no," I think of Monique. One day after class she took a deep breath, sighed, and told me she was exhausted. She complained that everyone at her job kept bringing her tasks to do. As a result, she had virtually no social life, and she was falling behind in college. She wanted advice on how to manage her time better.

> If you go to somebody and say, "I need help," they'll say, "Sure, honey, I wish I could," but if you say, "I need you to call so-and-so on Tuesday, will you do that?" they either will say yes or they'll say no. If they say no, you thank them and say, "Do you know someone who will?" If they say yes, you call on Wednesday to see if they did it. You wouldn't believe how good I've gotten at this, and I never knew how to ask anybody for anything before.
>
> *Barbara Sher*

"Sounds like you're working 60 hours a week and doing the work of two people," I observed. She nodded modestly. "Here's an outrageous thought: The next time someone at work brings you more to do, say 'no.'"

"That sounds so rude."

"Okay then, say, 'I'm sorry, but my schedule is full, and I won't be able to do that.'"

"What if my boss asks? I can't say 'no' to her."

"You can say, 'I'll be glad to take that on. But since I have so many projects already, I'll need you to give one of them to someone else. That way I'll have time to do a good job on this new project.'"

Monique agreed to experiment with saying "no." The next time I saw her, she was excited. "I sent my boss a memo telling her I had too much work and I couldn't take on the latest project she had assigned me. Before I'd even talked to her about the memo, one of my coworkers came by. He said our boss had sent him to take over some of my projects. Not only did I not get the new project, I got rid of two others. I just might be able to finish this semester after all."

Monique's voice had a power that hadn't been there before. With one "no" she had transformed herself from exhausted to exhilarated. That's the power of a Creator being assertive.

> When two people are relating maturely, each will be able to ask the other for what he or she wants or needs, fully trusting that the other will say "no" if he or she does not want to give it.
>
> *Edward Deci*

Journal Entry 20

In this activity, you will explore assertiveness. This powerful way of being creates great results, strengthens relationships, and builds self-esteem.

1. **Make a choice: Write about one of the following (A or B):**

    A. **Write three different responses to the instructor described in the following situation.** Respond to the instructor by (1) placating, (2) blaming, and (3) leveling. For an example of this exercise, refer to the dialogues on page 170.

    Situation: You register for a course required in your major. It is the last course you need to graduate. When you go to the first class meeting, the instructor tells you that your name is NOT on the roster. The course is full, and no other sections of the course are being offered. You've been shut out of the class. The instructor tells you that you'll have to postpone graduation and return next semester to complete this required course.

    Remember, in each of your three responses, you are writing what you would actually say to the instructor—first as a placator, second as a blamer, and third as a leveler.

    B. **Think about one of your most challenging academic goals. Decide who could help you with this goal. Write a letter to this person and request assistance.** You can decide later whether or not you will send the letter.

Recognizing When You Are Off Course

 **Focus Questions** In which of your life roles are you off course? Do you know how you got there? More important, do you know how to get back on course to your desired outcomes and experiences?

Take a deep breath, relax, and consider your journey so far.

You began by accepting personal responsibility for creating your life as you want it. Then you chose personally motivating goals and dreams that give purpose and direction to your life.

Next, you created a self-management plan and began taking effective actions. Most recently, you developed mutually supportive relationships to help you on your journey. Throughout, you have examined how to believe in yourself.

Despite all these efforts, you may still be off course—in college, in a relationship, in your job, or somewhere else in your life. You just aren't achieving your desired outcomes and experiences. Once again, you have an important choice to make. You can listen to the blaming, complaining, and excusing of your Inner Critic and Inner Defender. Or you can ask your Inner Guide to find answers to important questions such as . . .

- What habits do I have that sabotage my success?
- What beliefs do I have that get me off course?
- How can I consistently make wise choices that will create a rich, personally fulfilling life?

> Consider this: If at first you don't succeed, something is blocking your way.
>
> *Michael Ray & Rochelle Myers*

THE MYSTERY OF SELF-SABOTAGE

Self-sabotage has probably happened to everyone who's set off on a journey to a better life. Consider my student Jerome. Fresh from high school, Jerome said his dream was to start his own accounting firm by his 30th birthday. He set long-term goals of getting his college degree and passing the C.P.A. (certified public accountant) exam. He set short-term goals of earning A's in every class he took during his first semester. He developed a written self-management system and demonstrated interdependence by starting a study group. But at semester's end, the unthinkable happened: Jerome failed Accounting 101!

Wait a minute, though. Jerome's Inner Guide has more information. You see, Jerome made some strange choices during his first semester. He skipped his accounting class three times to work at a part-time job. On another day, he didn't attend class because he was angry with his girlfriend. Then he missed two Monday classes when he was hungover from weekend parties. He was late five times because parking was difficult to find. Jerome regularly put off doing homework until the last minute because he was so busy. He didn't hand in an

> Progressively we discover that there are levels of experience beneath the surface, beneath our consciousness, and we realize that these may hold the key both to the problems and the potentialities of our life.
>
> *Ira Progoff*

important assignment because he found it confusing. And he stopped going to his study group after the first meeting because ... well, he wasn't quite sure why. As the semester progressed, Jerome's anxiety about the final exam grew. The night before, he stayed up late cramming, then went to the exam exhausted. During the test, his mind went blank.

Haven't you, too, made choices that worked against your goals and dreams? Haven't we all! We take our eyes off the path for just a moment, and some invisible force comes along and pulls us off course. By the time we realize what's happened—if, in fact, we ever do—we can be miles off course and feeling miserable.

What's going on around here, anyway?

UNCONSCIOUS FORCES

One of the most important discoveries in psychology is the existence and power of unconscious forces in our lives. We now know that experiences from our past linger in our unconscious minds long after our conscious minds have forgotten them. As a result, we're influenced in our daily choices by old experiences we don't even recall.

Dr. Wilder Penfield of the Montreal Neurological Institute found evidence that our brains may retain nearly every experience we have ever had. Dr. Penfield performed brain surgery on patients who had local anesthesia but were otherwise fully awake. During the operation, he stimulated brain cells using a weak electric current. At that moment his patients reported re-experiencing long-forgotten events in vivid detail.

Further research by neuroscientist Joseph LeDoux suggests that a part of our brains called the amygdala stores emotionally charged but now unconscious memories. The amygdala, like a nervous watchman, examines every present experience and compares it to past experiences. When a key feature of a present event is similar to a distressing event from the past, it declares a match. Then, *without our conscious knowledge*, the amygdala hijacks our rational thought processes. It causes us to respond to the present event as we learned to respond to the past event. The problem is, the outdated response is often totally inappropriate in our present situation. By the time the amygdala loosens its grip on our decision-making power, we may have made some very bad choices.

If many of the forces that get us off course are unconscious, how can we spot their sabotaging influence? By analogy, the answer appears in a fascinating discovery in astronomy. Years ago, astronomers developed a mathematical formula to predict the orbit of any planet around the sun. However, one planet, Uranus, failed to follow its predicted orbit. Astronomers were baffled as to why Uranus was "off course." Then the French astronomer Leverrier proposed an ingenious explanation: The gravitational pull of an invisible planet was getting Uranus off course. Sure enough, when stronger telescopes were invented, the planet Neptune was discovered, and Leverrier was proven correct.

In the entire history of science, it is hard to find a discovery of comparable consequence to the discovery of the power of unconscious belief as a gateway—or an obstacle—to the hidden mind, and its untapped potentialities.

Willis Harman

We know from surgical experiences that electrical stimulation delivered to the temporal area of the brain elicits images of events that occurred in the patient's past. This is confirmation that such memories are "stored," but in most instances they cannot be voluntarily recollected. Thus, all of us "know" more than we are aware that we know.

Richard Restak, M.D.

Here's the point: Like planets, we all have invisible Neptunes tugging at us every day. For us, these invisible forces are not in outer space. They exist in inner space, in our unconscious minds. As with Uranus, the first clue to spotting the existence of these unconscious forces is recognizing that we are off course. So, be candid. Where are you off course in your life today? School? Relationships? Work? Health? Finances? Elsewhere? What desired outcomes and experiences are you moving away from instead of toward? What goals and dreams seem to be slipping away? Self-awareness allows you to identify that you are off course. Only then can you start making wiser choices that will get you back on course to the life you want to create.

> I learned that I could not look to my exterior self to do anything for me. If I was going to accomplish anything in life I had to start from within.
>
> *Oprah Winfrey*

Journal Entry 21

Everyone gets off course at times, but only those who are self-aware can make a course correction to improve their lives.

1. **Write about a time when you were off course and took effective actions to get back on course.** Examples include ending an unhealthy relationship, entering college years after high school, changing careers, stopping an addiction, choosing to be more assertive, or changing a negative belief or bias you held about yourself, other people, or the world. Dive deep in your journal entry by asking and answering questions such as the following:
- In what area of my life was I off course?
- What choices had I made to get off course?
- What changes did I make to get back on course?
- What challenges did I face while making this change?
- What personal strengths helped me make this change?
- What benefits did I experience as a result of my change?
- If I hadn't made this change, what would my life be like today?

2. **Write about an area of your life in which you are off course today.** If you need help in identifying an area, review your desired outcomes and experiences from Journal Entry 9 and your goals and dreams from Journal Entry 10. Explain which area of your life is furthest from the way you would like it to be. What choices have you made that got you off course? What will be the effect on your life if you continue to stay off course?

The fact that you've made positive changes in the past is a good reminder that you have the personal strengths to make similar changes whenever you wish. All you need is the awareness that you're off course and the motivation to make new choices.

> The truth is that our finest moments are most likely to occur when we are feeling deeply uncomfortable, unhappy, or unfulfilled. For it is only in such moments, propelled by our discomfort, that we are likely to step out of our ruts and start searching for different ways or truer answers.
>
> *M. Scott Peck, M.D.*

One Student's Story

SARAH RICHMOND
Missouri University of Science and Technology, Missouri

I was in the emergency room when it hit me how far off course I was. My friend Matt had driven me to the emergency room because the Student Health Center couldn't supply the antibiotics I needed for a bad sore throat. As we sat in the waiting room talking, I told Matt that I was failing math, and I broke down and cried. I told him I was doing things in college that I had never done at home. When I was in high school, my parents were very strict. They didn't let me go out late during the week, and they'd wake me up in the morning to make sure I went to school. But in college, no one cares if you stay out all night or even if you get up and go to class. I had adopted "Why not?" as my motto, and I started doing things I knew I shouldn't be doing. My weekends had become a blur of boys and parties, and I had even started partying during the week. The parties I went to in high school were mostly small girls' nights, nothing like the drunken fraternity parties I was going to on campus. In high school I was one of the smart kids, and even though I hardly ever studied, I was an honor student. But college was different. I was doing terrible in math and not much better in biology. It was a shock to not do as well as I had in high school.

I started getting a bleak outlook on life, and I didn't really want to be at the university. I had no idea what I wanted to major in. I thought of myself as lazy and irresponsible. I remember telling one of my friends that I should just get married, have kids, and then I'd probably be divorced by 40. After that I'd spend the rest of my life in a lousy job, struggling to survive. I felt like I couldn't do anything right. I don't know why I let everything bother me so much, but I felt awful.

Talking with Matt in the emergency room, I started realizing how lonely I felt in college. I missed my family, especially my sister. I wasn't getting along with my roommate, and we competed about everything: going out, boys, drinking, staying up late, playing video games, you name it. A lot of the students at my university are really into playing *Halo*. I tried to fit in, but I'm no good at video games. At my school, if you're not in engineering, they tease you non-stop. One time a guy picked up my *On Course* book and starting teasing me about the class. "So what do you do in that class," he asked, "sit around and talk about your *feelings*?" I didn't bother saying that the course helped me think things out, things I wouldn't have thought about, like all of the mistakes I was making.

That day in the emergency room was my wake up call. Sitting there talking with Matt, I not only realized that I was way off course, I also realized that deep down I didn't believe in myself, and therefore I couldn't take actions today to improve my tomorrow. After that, I realized I had to make some dramatic changes. I got a new roommate, stopped partying, buckled down, and passed my math class. That was two years ago. Today I'm a junior and my life is very different. I've found a major that I love, I just finished an internship that was great, and my GPA is 3.4. Making positive changes isn't always easy. But my life started to get better that day in the emergency room when I took a good look at myself and realized just how far off course I was.

Photo: Courtesy of Sarah Richmond

Identifying Your Scripts

 **Focus Questions** What habit patterns in your life get you off course? How did these habit patterns develop?

Once you realize you're off course, you need to figure out how to get back on course. This can be tricky. The forces pulling us off course are often just as invisible to us as the planet Neptune was to Leverrier and his fellow observers of outer space.

As observers of inner space, psychologists seek to identify what they can't actually see: the internal forces that divert human potential into disappointment. In various psychological theories, these unconscious inner forces have been called names such as ego defenses, conditioned responses, programs, mental tapes, blind spots, schemas, and life-traps.

The term I like best to describe our unconscious internal forces was coined by psychologist Eric Berne: **scripts**. In the world of theater, a script tells an actor what words, actions, and emotions to perform onstage. When the actor gets a cue from others in the play, he doesn't make a choice about his response. He responds automatically as his script directs. Performance after performance, he reacts the same way to the same cues.

Responding automatically from a dramatic script is one sure way to succeed as an actor. However, responding automatically from a *life* script is one sure way to struggle as a human being.

ANATOMY OF A SCRIPT

Everyone has scripts. I do, your instructors do, your classmates do, you do. Some scripts have helped us achieve our present success. Other scripts may be getting us off course from our goals and dreams. Becoming aware of our unique personal scripts helps us make wise choices at each fork in the road, choices that help us create the life we want.

Scripts are composed of two parts. Closest to the surface of our awareness reside the directions for how we are to think, feel, and behave. **Thought patterns** include habitual self-talk such as *I'm too busy, I'm good at math, People different from me are a threat, I always screw up, The way we do things around here is the right way so all other ways must be wrong, I can't write*. **Emotional patterns** include habitual feelings such as anger, excitement, anxiety, sadness, and joy. **Behavior patterns** include habitual actions such as smoking cigarettes, criticizing others, arriving on time, never asking for help, and exercising regularly. When people know us well, they can often predict what we will say, feel, or do in a given situation. This ability reveals their recognition of our patterns.

Deeper in our unconscious mind lies the second, and more elusive, part of our scripts, our **core beliefs**. Early in life, we form core beliefs about the world (e.g., *The world is safe* or *The world is dangerous*), about other people (e.g., *People can be trusted* or *People can't be trusted*), and about ourselves (e.g., *I'm worthy* or *I'm unworthy*). Though we're seldom aware of our core beliefs, these unconscious judgments dictate what we consistently think, feel, and do. These beliefs become the lenses through which we see the world. Whether accurate or distorted, our beliefs dictate the choices we make at each fork in the road. What do you believe that

> A psychological script is a person's ongoing program for his life drama which dictates where he is going with his life and how he is to get there. It is a drama he compulsively acts out, though his awareness of it may be vague.
>
> Muriel James &
> Dorothy Jongeward

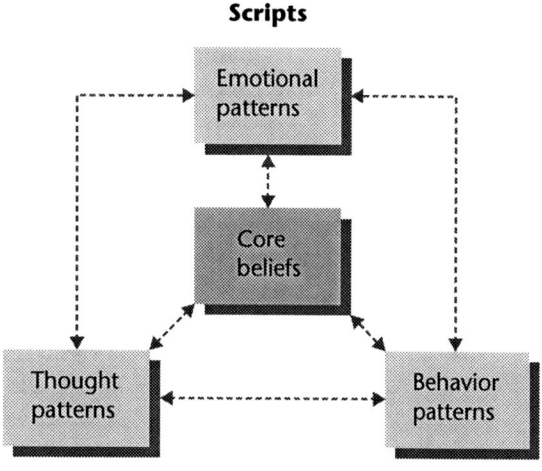

causes you to make choices that other people think are strange? More important, what do you believe that keeps you from creating the outcomes and experiences you want?

HOW WE WROTE OUR SCRIPTS

Though no one knows exactly how we wrote our life scripts as children, reasonable explanations exist. One factor seems to be **how others responded to us**. Imagine this scene: You're two years old. You're feeling lonely and hungry, and you begin to cry. Your mother hurries in to pick you up. "There, there," she croons. "It's all right." She hugs you, feeds you, sings to you. You fall asleep full and content. If this happens often enough, what do you suppose you'd decide about the world, about other people, about yourself? Probably you'd believe *The world is kind; People will help me; I am lovable*. In turn, these beliefs would dictate your thoughts, emotions, and behaviors. With positive beliefs such as these at the core of your scripts, very likely you'd develop optimistic thought patterns (e.g., *If I ask, I'll get help*), positive emotional patterns (e.g., joy and enthusiasm), and empowering behavior patterns (e.g., asking for what you want).

Now imagine the same childhood scene with a different response. You cry but no one comes. You scream louder, but still no one comes. Finally you abandon hope that anyone will respond. You cry yourself to sleep, alone and hungry. Imagine also that being ignored happens often. You'd probably develop core beliefs such as *The world doesn't care about me; People won't help me; I'm not important*. You could very well develop pessimistic thought patterns (e.g., *I'm alone*), negative emotional patterns (e.g., anxiety and anger), and passive behavior patterns (e.g., not asking for what you want).

Now, imagine this scene one more time. As you're crying for attention and food, an adult storms into your room, screams "Shut up!" and slaps your face. After a few wounding experiences like this, you may decide *The world is a dangerous and painful place; People will hurt me; I'm unlovable!* These beliefs may lead to defensive thought patterns (e.g., *People are out to get me*), defensive emotional patterns (e.g., fear and rage), and defensive behavior patterns (e.g., immediately fighting or fleeing at the first sign of danger). Imagine how easily these patterns could get you off course later in life.

A second factor that seems to shape our scripts is **what significant adults said to us**. What did they say about the world: Is it safe or dangerous? What did they say about other people, especially those who are different from us: Can they be trusted or not? And, perhaps most important, what did important adults say about us? Psychologists have a term for qualities that tell us how we "are" or "should be": **attributions**. Common attributions tell us to be *good, quiet, rebellious, devoted, helpful, athletic, sexy, tough, independent, dependent, invisible, macho, dominant, competitive, smart, shy,* or *confident*.

Psychologists also have a term for the qualities that tell us what we "are not" or "should not be": **injunctions**. Common injunctions include *don't be yourself,*

> Parents, deliberately or unaware, teach their children from birth how to behave, think, feel, and perceive. Liberation from these influences is no easy matter.
>
> *Eric Berne*

> The hearts of small children are delicate organs. A cruel beginning in this world can twist them into curious shapes. The heart of a hurt child can shrink so that forever afterward it is hard and pitted as the seed of a peach.
>
> *Carson McCullers*

don't talk back, don't feel, don't think, don't be intimate, don't say no, don't say yes, don't get angry, don't trust people who are different from you, don't show your feelings, don't love yourself, don't be happy, don't be weak, don't believe in yourself, don't exist.

A third way we seem to write our scripts is by **observing the behavior of significant adults**. Children notice, *What did important adults do? If it's right for them, it's right for me.* When children play, we see them trying on adult behaviors, conversations, and emotions. It doesn't take a detective to figure out where they learned them. From significant adults we learn not only our unique personal scripts but our cultural programs as well. For example, some cultures believe we shape our future through our choices, whereas other cultures believe our future is determined by forces beyond our control. Some cultures place emphasis on future accomplishments, whereas others focus on the present or past. Some cultures are very time conscious, whereas others are more casual about time. Some cultures encourage individuality, whereas others place family and community above all other concerns. Each belief is deeply imbedded in the culture and becomes the lens through which its members see the world, influencing their choices, whether they are aware of the beliefs or not.

In these ways we each develop our personal scripts and cultural programs. Each is comprised of core beliefs and their resulting patterns of thoughts, feelings, and behaviors. At critical choice points, especially when we are under stress, we unconsciously default to our personal scripts and cultural programs for guidance.

The good news about our unconscious scripts and programs is that their intention is always positive—always to minimize our pain, always to maximize our pleasure. They help us adapt to the family and society in which we are born. Many of us made it through the mental, emotional, and physical challenges of growing up with the help of our childhood scripts and programs. Some of us would not have survived without them.

But, as you might guess, there is bad news as well: When we make unconscious choices as adults, we often get off course. That's because the scripts and programs we developed in childhood often do not apply to the situations of our present lives. Imagine an adult who can't stop playing a role he or she learned years ago for a grade school play! Many of us do the equivalent of this in our daily lives.

To others, a choice I make may seem strange. To me, it makes perfect sense. The important issue, though, is: Do my habitual choices help or hinder me in the pursuit of the life I want to create? To answer this question, I need to take three steps. First, I need to become aware of my Neptunes, that is, my unconscious beliefs, attitudes, biases, norms, prejudices, and values. Second, I need to assess which of my mindsets help and which hinder me in the pursuit of my goals and dreams. And finally, I need to keep and strengthen the habits that help me while revising or replacing the ones that hinder me. And it all starts with self-awareness.

By the time we are adults, we have learned many cultural rules of behavior and have practiced those rules so much that they are second nature to us. Much of our behavior as adults is influenced by these learned patterns and rules, and we are so well practiced at them that we engage in these behaviors automatically and unconsciously.

David Matsumoto and Linda Juang

The more you are keenly aware of your misery-creating thoughts, feelings, and behaviors, the greater your chances are of ridding yourself of them.

Albert Ellis

SELF-DEFEATING HABIT PATTERNS

Though our unconscious scripts are as invisible to us as the planet Neptune was to early astronomers, we can often see their influence in our lives. Put a check next to any of the following patterns of thought, emotion, and behavior that are often true of you. These habits may reveal the presence of personal scripts or cultural programs that get you off course. In particular, see if you can identify any habits that may have gotten you off course in the area you wrote about in Journal Entry 21.

> The grooves of mindlessness run deep. We know our scripts by heart.
>
> *Ellen J. Langer*

☐ 1. I waste a lot of time doing unimportant things (e.g., television, video games).
☐ 2. I wonder if I'm "college material."
☐ 3. I easily get upset (e.g., angry, sad, anxious, depressed, guilty, frustrated).
☐ 4. I hang out with people who don't support my academic goals.
☐ 5. I believe that most people don't like me.
☐ 6. I often turn in college assignments late.
☐ 7. I worry that people stereotype me because of a cultural group (race, religion, sex, economic class, age, etc.) to which I belong rather than seeing me for who I really am.
☐ 8. I worry excessively about doing things perfectly.
☐ 9. I think most of my classmates are smarter than I am.
☐ 10. I quit on things that are important to me.
☐ 11. I allow a person in my life to treat me badly.
☐ 12. I don't believe I deserve success as much as other people do.
☐ 13. I miss more college classes than I should.
☐ 14. I'm very critical of myself.
☐ 15. I wait until the last minute to do important college assignments.
☐ 16. I don't ask questions in class or participate in class discussions.
☐ 17. I often break promises I have made to myself or others.
☐ 18. I am addicted to something (e.g., caffeine, alcohol, cigarettes, soft drinks, video games, social networking Internet sites, drugs).
☐ 19. I experience severe test anxiety.
☐ 20. I feel uncomfortable about asking for help.
☐ 21. I have strong negative feelings about a particular group of people who are different from me.
☐ 22. I often side-talk or daydream in my college classes.
☐ 23. I seldom do my best work on college assignments.
☐ 24. I am very critical of other people.
☐ 25. I get extremely nervous when I speak to a group.

> What lies behind us and what lies before us are tiny matters compared to what lies within us.
>
> *Oliver Wendell Holmes*

- ☐ **26.** I keep promising to study more in college, but I don't.
- ☐ **27.** I get my feelings hurt easily.
- ☐ **28.** I am a loner.
- ☐ **29.** I am uncomfortable being around people who are different from me.
- ☐ **30.** I get defensive when someone gives me feedback that I did something wrong.
- ☐ **31.** I . . . _____
- ☐ **32.** I . . . _____

Are you aware of any other of your patterns—mental, emotional, or behavioral? If so, add them to the list.

> It is not true that life is one damn thing after another—it's one damn thing over and over.
>
> *Edna St. Vincent Millay, American poet*

Journal Entry 22

In this activity, you will explore self-defeating patterns in your life that may reveal unconscious scripts. You're about to embark on an exciting journey into your inner world! There you can discover—and later revise—the invisible forces that have gotten you off course from your goals and dreams.

1. **Write about one of your self-defeating *behavior* patterns.** Choose a behavior pattern that you checked on the list or identify a self-defeating behavior that isn't on the list but that you do often. Remember, a behavior is something someone else can see you do. Develop your journal paragraphs by anticipating questions that someone reading it might have about this behavior pattern. (Even you might have questions when you read your journal 10 years from now.) For example,

- What exactly is your self-defeating behavior pattern?
- What are some specific examples of when you did this behavior?
- What may have caused this habit?
- What undesirable effects has it had on your life?
- How would your life be improved if you changed it?

One student began by writing, One of my self-defeating behavior patterns is that I seldom do my best work on college assignments. For example, in my biology lab. . . .

2. **Repeat Step 1 for one of your self-defeating *thought* patterns or for one of your self-defeating *emotional* patterns.** Once again, choose a pattern that you checked on the list or identify a habit that isn't on the list but that you often think or feel. You might begin, *One of my self-defeating thought patterns is that I often wonder if I am smart enough to be successful in college. I especially think this during exams. For example, last Thursday I . . . Or . . . One of my self-defeating emotional patterns is that I often feel frustrated. For example. . . .*

> All serious daring starts from within.
>
> *Eudora Welty*

One Student's Story

JAMES FLORIOLLI
Foothill College, California

At different points in my life I've given up when I ran into a challenge. As a child, I loved baseball, but when I got hit in the face with a ball, I stopped playing. In school, I started having problems with my writing skills, and I was diagnosed with a learning disability. I got all kinds of accommodations, even more than I deserved, and I started goofing off. I convinced myself that success was getting the best grades possible with the least amount of work. After high school, college didn't seem like a viable option, so I joined the Marine Corps Reserve. Boot camp was even harder than I thought it would be. Once again, I used the minimum amount of effort necessary to complete each task, and I failed to achieve the level of success in the Marines that I could have. When I left the Marines to get a civilian job, I defined success as getting maximum compensation for minimum effort.

I got a job at the phone company and at first it seemed perfect. I'm very well paid for very little effort. However, this situation isn't as rewarding as I thought it would be. After a few years I began to want a greater challenge. I knew I needed an education to advance in the workplace, so I started taking college courses part-time. For the first year I avoided classes that involved a lot of writing, as I was still intimidated by past failures in this area. But when poor writing began to affect my grades in other courses, I decided to take a composition class. In that class we read *On Course*, and in the chapter about self-awareness, I began to see how negative scripts could cause problems. I started wondering if there was a script contributing to the frustration I was feeling in my life. An idea kept coming up that at first I was unwilling to accept. I had always thought of myself as a hard worker, but looking back on my life I could not deny there were challenges I had run away from. When baseball had required extra work to get past my fear of the ball, I quit. When school stopped coming easily to me, I quit. When I realized how hard I'd have to work to be a success in the Marines, I quit. Seeing this pattern was powerful for me. Finally, I felt like I understood how I ended up in the situation I am in. I realized that I'll do anything to avoid feeling bad. If I feel down in any way, I'm willing to throw everything out the window to feel better. In the past, I have doubted myself and been afraid to take risks. I overvalued security and undervalued me. I need to believe I am capable of accomplishing anything I want to.

Soon I have to pick my college major. One option is to get a computer science degree and continue working at the phone company. This would probably lead to the greatest profit and security. Or, I could choose a major that would prepare me for my dream job working in the front office of a professional baseball team. Obviously, going for my dream would be very difficult and call for a large initial pay cut. Knowing I have an issue with not following through on my most challenging commitments, I need to set my goals very carefully. No matter what I choose, I hope that when everything is said and done I will be proud of what I have accomplished. This will mean I have successfully revised my negative script of running from important challenges in my life.

Rewriting Your Outdated Scripts

Focus Question How can you revise the self-defeating scripts that keep you from achieving your full potential?

Once in a writing class, I was explaining how to organize an essay when a student named Diana told me she didn't understand. She asked if I'd write an explanation on the board.

Earlier in the class, we'd been talking about the differences between left-brain and right-brain thinking. We'd discussed how the left side of the brain deals with logical, organized information, while the right side deals with more creative, intuitive concepts. "No problem," I said to Diana, "I hear your left brain crying out for some order. Let's see if I can help."

As I turned to write on the blackboard, she screamed, "You have no right to talk to me that way!"

I was stunned. Talk about a strange response! I took a deep breath to compose myself. "Maybe we could talk about this after class," I said.

THE IMPACT OF OUTDATED BELIEFS

Diana and I did talk, and I learned that she was in her late 30s, a single mother of an 8-year-old daughter. Our conversation wandered for a while; then Diana mentioned that she had always disliked school. In elementary school, she had consistently gotten low grades, while her sister consistently earned A's. One day, when Diana was about 12, she overheard her father and mother talking about her poor report card. "I don't know what we're going to do with Diana," her father said. "She's the *half-brain* of the family." [Do you see it yet . . . what got Diana upset with me?]

Diana accepted as a fact other people's belief that she couldn't think or learn. She developed patterns of thoughts, emotions, and behaviors that supported this belief. She decided that school was a waste of time (thought), she exploded when anyone questioned her about schoolwork (emotion), and she was often absent (behavior). Diana barely graduated from high school, then got a menial job that bored her.

For nearly 20 years, Diana heard her Inner Critic (sounding much like her father) telling her that something was wrong with her brain. Finally, another inner voice began to whisper, *Maybe—just maybe. . . .* Then one day she took a big risk and enrolled in college.

"So what happens?" she said, getting angry again. "I get a teacher who calls me a *half-brain*! I knew this would happen. I ought to just quit."

I used my best active listening skills: I listened to understand. I reflected both her thoughts and her anger. I asked her to clarify and expand. I allowed long periods of silence.

Finally, her emotional storm subsided. She took a deep breath and sat back.

I waited a few moments. "Diana, I know you think I called you a 'half-brain.' But what I actually said was *left* brain. Remember we had been talking in class about the difference between left-brain and right-brain thinking? Two different approaches to planning your essay? I was talking about that."

"But I *heard* you!"

"I know that's what you *heard*. But that isn't what I *said*. I've read two of your essays, and I know your brain works just fine. What really matters, though, is what *you* think! You need to believe in your own intelligence. Otherwise, you'll always be ready to hear people call you a 'half-brain' no matter what they really said. Worse, you'll always believe it yourself."

> We don't see things as they are, we see them as we are.
>
> *Anais Nin*

> We are what we think.
> All that we are arises
> With our thoughts.
> With our thoughts,
> We make the world.
>
> *The Buddha*

Diana had come within an inch of dropping out of college, of abandoning her dreams of a college degree. And all because of her childhood script.

DOING THE REWRITE

Until we revise our limiting scripts, we're less likely to achieve some of our most cherished goals and dreams. That's why realizing we're off course can be a blessing in disguise. By identifying the self-defeating patterns of thought, emotion, and behavior that got us off course, we may be able to discover and revise the underlying core beliefs that are sabotaging our success.

Diana stuck it out and passed English 101. She persevered and graduated with an Associate of Arts degree in early childhood education. When I spoke to her last, she was working at a nursery school and talking about returning to college to finish her bachelor's degree. Like most of us, she'll probably be in a tug of war with her scripts for the rest of her life. But now, at least, she knows that she, and not her scripts, can be in charge of making her choices.

One of the great discoveries about the human condition is this: We are not stuck with our personal scripts or cultural programming. We can re-create ourselves. We can keep what works and change what doesn't. By revising outdated scripts, we can get back on course and dramatically improve the outcomes and experiences of our lives.

> In developing our own self-awareness many of us discover ineffective scripts, deeply embedded habits that are totally unworthy of us, totally incongruent with the things we really value in life.
>
> Stephen Covey

In this activity, you'll practice revising your scripts, thus taking greater control of your life. As in Journal Entry 18, you'll once again be writing a conversation with your Inner Guide, a critical thinking skill that empowers you to become your own best coach, counselor, mentor, and guide through challenging times. This practical application of critical thinking greatly enhances your self-awareness, helping you take greater responsibility for making the wise choices necessary to create your desired outcomes and experiences.

1. Write a dialogue with your Inner Guide that will help you revise your self-sabotaging scripts.

    Have your Inner Guide ask you the following 10 questions. After answering each question, let your Inner Guide use one or more of the active listening skills to help you dive deeper:

    1. **Silence** (demonstrating that you are paying close attention to the speaker)
    2. **Reflection** (expressing in your own words what you think the speaker is saying and feeling)

3. **Expansion** (requesting examples, evidence, and experiences)
4. **Clarification** (asking for an explanation)

Ten questions from Your Inner Guide:

1. In what area of your life are you off course?
2. What self-defeating **thought patterns** of yours may have contributed to this situation?
3. What different thoughts could you choose to get back on course?
4. What self-defeating **emotional patterns** of yours may have contributed to this situation?
5. What different emotions could you choose to get back on course?
6. What self-defeating **behavior patterns** of yours may have contributed to this situation?
7. What different behaviors could you choose to get back on course?
8. What limiting **core beliefs** of yours (about the world, other people, or yourself) may have led you to adopt the self-defeating patterns that we've been discussing?
9. What different beliefs could you choose to get back on course?
10. As a result of what you've learned here, what new behaviors, thoughts, emotions, or core beliefs will you adopt?

A sample dialogue follows.

Sample Dialogue with Your Inner Guide

IG: In what area of your life are you off course? (Question 1)
ME: My grades are terrible this semester.
IG: Would you say more about that? **(Expansion)**
ME: In high school I got mostly A's and B's even though I played three sports. My goal this semester is to have at least a 3.5 grade point average, but the way things are going, I'll be lucky if I even get a 2.0.
IG: What self-defeating **thought patterns** of yours may have contributed to this situation? (Question 2)
ME: I guess I tell myself I shouldn't have to work hard to get good grades in college.
IG: Why do you think that? Is there a deeper meaning? **(Clarification)**
ME: If I have to study hard, then I must not be very smart.
IG: That's a good awareness! What different thoughts could you choose to get back on course to your goal of getting at least a 3.5 average? (Question 3)
ME: I could remind myself that going to college is like moving from the minor leagues to the major leagues. The challenge is a lot greater,

> It is a marvelous faculty of the human mind that we are also able to stop old programming from holding us back, anytime we choose to. That gift is called conscious choice.
>
> *Shad Helmstetter*

> Until you make the unconscious conscious, it will direct your life and you will call it fate.
>
> *Carl Jung*

Journal Entry 23 *continued*

and I better start studying like a major league student or I'm not going to succeed.

IG: What self-defeating **emotional patterns** of yours may have contributed to this situation? (Question 4)

ME: I get really frustrated when I don't understand something right away.

IG: So you want to understand it immediately. **(Reflection)**

ME: Absolutely. When I don't get it right away, I switch to something else.

IG: That's understandable since everything came so easy to you in high school. What different emotion could you choose to get you back on course to your goal of a 3.5 GPA? (Question 5)

ME: I could do the same thing I do in basketball when the coach asks me to shut down the other team's top scorer. I can psych myself up and push myself to study harder. My college degree is worth a lot more to me than winning a basketball game.

IG: What self-defeating **behavior patterns** of yours may have contributed to this situation? (Question 6)

ME: Like I said before, I get frustrated when I don't understand something right away, and then I put it aside. I always plan to come back to it later, but usually I don't.

IG: Are there any other self-defeating behaviors you can think of? **(Expansion)**

ME: I don't ask my teachers for help or go to the tutoring center either. I guess I hate asking for help. It's like admitting that I'm not very smart.

IG: There's that concern again about not being smart enough. **(Reflection)**

ME: I hadn't realized my Inner Critic is so loud!

IG: Now you can prove your Inner Critic wrong. What different behaviors could you choose to get back on course to your goal? (Question 7)

ME: I could ask my teachers for more help and go to the tutoring center. Also, when I set homework aside, I could write on my calendar when I'm going to work on it again. I'm really good about doing things that I write down.

IG: I like it! What limiting **core beliefs** of yours (about the world, other people, or yourself) may have led you to adopt the self-defeating patterns that we've been discussing? (Question 8)

ME: This conversation has made me realize I have some doubts about whether I'm as smart as I think I am. Maybe I don't believe I can really succeed in college unless studying comes easy for me. Maybe I got a little spoiled and lazy in high school.

IG: What different core belief could you choose to get back on course to your goal? (Question 9)

ME: I can succeed in college if I'm willing to do the work...and give it my best.

> Whatever we believe about ourselves and our ability comes true for us.
>
> *Susan L. Taylor, editor-in-chief, Essence Magazine*

IG: That's great! Do the work and do your best! As a result of what you've learned here, what new behaviors, thoughts, emotions, or core beliefs will you commit to? (Question 10)

ME: When I feel like putting an assignment aside, I'll work on it for at least 15 more minutes. Then, if I stop before I'm finished, I'll write on my calendar when I'm going to work on it again and I'll go back and finish it later. If I'm still having trouble with the assignment, I'll ask my professor for help. And I'll keep reminding myself, "Do the work and do my best." If that doesn't help, I'll be back to talk to you some more. I *will* get a 3.5 average! Thanks for listening.

CALVIN and HOBBES © 1990, Watterson. Dist. by Universal UCLICK. Reprinted with. All rights reserved.

BELIEVING IN YOURSELF

Write Your Own Rules

 **Focus Questions** What personal rules do you have that dictate the choices you make daily? Which of these rules help you create high self-esteem?

Few things affect self-esteem more than our sense of personal power. When we feel like mere passengers in life, with no apparent choice in where we're going, self-esteem shrivels. When we feel like the pilots of our lives, with the power to choose wisely and reach our goals and dream, self-esteem grows.

Unconscious personal scripts and cultural programs can steal our sense of personal power and drag down our self-esteem. When these unconscious forces take over, we essentially give up control of our lives. Then we make those strange choices that can push us far off course and leave us wondering, "How the heck did I get over here?" Consider, for example, the cultural tradition of *marianism* in which Latinas are expected to follow rules such as these: *Place the needs of your husband and family above your own, Never criticize your husband, Remain faithful to your marriage regardless of the cost, Never share personal problems with others.* If a Latina has consciously accepted these rules as her own, she will gladly make the personal sacrifices needed, and she will achieve the outcomes and experiences of her choosing. In fact, her sense of cultural pride may very well give her self-esteem a powerful boost. However, if she unconsciously lets these rules dictate her choices, she may feel helpless and angry at the life she is living. Imagine, for example, trying to earn a college degree if you are forever setting aside your dreams to help others achieve what they want. Only when you consciously accept, revise, or replace some cultural rules are you likely to feel completely at peace with yourself. The same, of course, is true of the rules embedded in your personal scripts.

As psychologist Virginia Satir pointed out, we are all living by rules, but the important issue is *Have we chosen our own rules*? To answer that question, you'll want to identify and preserve any empowering rules that are keeping you on course. Then you'll want to become conscious of and revise any rules that are holding you back. Finally, you'll want to write new rules that will support you in achieving even greater victories. That's what former first lady Eleanor Roosevelt did. Here are some of the life rules she created to guide her choices: *Do whatever comes your way as well as you can. Think as little as possible about yourself; think as much as possible about other people. Since you get more joy out of giving joy to others, you should put a good deal of thought in the happiness that you are able to give.*

I think you're going to be very surprised to discover that you may be living by rules of which you're not even aware.

Virginia Satir

As a member of the Sikh faith, I was constantly keeping track of so many rules: what to wear, what to eat, forbidden behaviors, and my duties to my family. When I added it all up, there wasn't much left for me to decide—so many of my decision had been made for me.

Sheena Iyengar

THREE SUCCESS RULES

I have polled thousands of college instructors, and they consistently identify three behaviors that their most successful students do consistently. As you'll see, these rules apply just as well to creating great outcomes in other life roles such as your career and relationships. Consider, then, these three rules as the foundation of your personal code of conduct.

Rule 1: I Show Up

Commit to attending every class from beginning to end. Someone once said that 90 percent of success is simply showing up. Makes sense, doesn't it? How can you be successful at something if you're not there? Studies show a direct correlation between attendance and grades (as one measure of success). At Baltimore City Community College, a study found that, on average, as absences went up, grades went down, especially in introductory courses. A study by a business professor at Arizona State University showed that, on average, his students' grades went down one full grade for every two classes they missed. If you can't get motivated to show up, maybe you need new goals and dreams.

Rule 2: I Do My Best Work

Commit to doing your best work on all assignments, including turning them in on time. You'd be amazed at how many sloppy assignments instructors see. But it isn't just students who are guilty. A friend in business has shown me hundreds of job applications so sloppily prepared that they begged to be tossed in the trash. Doing your best work on assignments is a rule that will propel you to success in all you do.

Rule 3: I Participate Actively

Commit to getting involved. College, like life, isn't a spectator sport. Come to class prepared. Listen attentively. Take notes. Think deeply about what's being said. Ask yourself how you can apply your course work to achieve your goals and dreams. Read ahead. Start a study group. Ask questions. Answer questions. If you participate at this high level, you couldn't keep yourself from learning even if you wanted to.

Some students resist adopting these three basic rules of success. They say, "But what if I get sick? What if my car breaks down on the way to class? What if . . .?" I trust that by now you recognize the voice of the Inner Defender, the internal excuse maker.

Of course something may happen to keep you from following your rules. Each rule is simply your strong *intention*. Each rule identifies an action you believe will help you achieve your desired outcomes and experiences. So you *intend* to be at every class from beginning to end. You *intend* to do your very best work and turn assignments in on time. You *intend* to participate actively. Your promise *to yourself* is never to break your own rules for a frivolous reason. However, you'll always break your own rules if something of a higher value (like

> The most important thing is to have a code of life, to know how to live.
>
> *Hans Selye, M.D.*

> People who lead a satisfying life, who are in tune with their past and with their future—in short, people whom we would call "happy"—are generally individuals who have lived their lives according to rules they themselves created.
>
> *Mihaly Csikszentmihalyi*

your health) demands it. At each fork in the road, the key to your success is being aware of which choice leads to the future you want. When you are a Creator, you make each choice uncontaminated by the past (your scripts), informed by your own rules of conduct, and ultimately determined by which option, in that moment, will best support the achievement of your goals and dreams.

Changing Your Habits

Exceptional students not only follow these three basic rules of success, they also create their own rules for college and life. By choosing personal rules, they commit to replacing their limiting scripts and cultural constraints with consciously chosen habits. Here are a few of my own life rules:

- I keep promises to myself and others.
- I seek feedback and make appropriate course corrections.
- I respect others by arriving on time.
- I do my very best work on all projects important to me.
- I play and create joy.
- I care for my body with exercise, healthy food, and good medical care.
- I am kind.

Do I follow these rules every day of my life? Unfortunately, no. And when I don't, I soon see myself getting off course. Then I can reelect to follow my self-chosen rules and avoid sabotaging the life I want to create.

Once we follow our own rules long enough, they're no longer simply rules. They become habits. And once our positive actions, thoughts, and feelings become habits, few obstacles can block the path to our success.

> What is hateful to you do not to your fellowman. That is the entire Law; all the rest is commentary.
>
> *The Talmud*

> I'll give you the Four Rules of Success:
> 1. Decide what you want.
> 2. Decide what you want to give up in order to get what you want.
> 3. Associate with successful people.
> 4. Plan your work and work your plan.
>
> Blair Underwood, actor

Journal Entry 24

In this activity, you will write your own rules for success in college and in life. By following your own code of conduct, you will more likely stay on course toward your greatest dreams.

To focus your mind, ask yourself, "What do successful people do consistently? What are their thoughts, attitudes, behaviors, and beliefs?"

1. Title a clean journal page "MY PERSONAL RULES FOR SUCCESS IN COLLEGE AND IN LIFE." Below that, write a list of your own rules for achieving your goals in college. List only those actions to which you're willing to commit to do consistently. You might want to print your rules on certificate paper and post them where you can see them daily (perhaps right next to your affirmation). Consider adopting the following as your first three rules:

Developing a Learning Orientation to Life

 **Focus Question** How can you maximize your learning in college and in life?

"Uh-oh," I thought. "I am in big trouble!"

I was 18 years old at the time, but I recall that scary moment as if it were yesterday. I was about to start my first semester in college. Our entire class was on campus for orientation, and one task was to choose our first-semester classes. I was sitting with one of my new roommates exploring course descriptions. John was going down the reading list for a literature course we were considering. "I've read this book," he said, ticking the title with the tip of his pen, "and this one . . . and this one. . . . and this one . . . and this one." Like many of my classmates, John had gone to a private high school. I had gone to a public high school. John had read

every book on the list. I had never even *heard* of the books on the list. That's when I thought: "Uh-oh . . . I am in big trouble!"

In that moment, I made an unconscious and unfortunate choice. I went into survival mode: *I just want to survive the next four years and graduate.* As a result, I filled my schedule with courses I thought would be easy. One course turned out to be more difficult than I thought, so I dropped it. During classes, I seldom spoke, afraid I would say something stupid. At the end of my first semester, I breathed a sigh of relief. I had passed all of my courses. My grades were much lower than they had been in high school, but I had survived. For the next seven semesters, I avoided taking classes with a professor who had a reputation of being "hard." When it came time to pick a major, I chose the one a friend told me was the easiest. My grades crept steadily upward as I got better and better at playing the grade game. After four years, I achieved my goal. I graduated. By most standards I was a success in college. But was I?

> Too many students are hung up on grades and on proving their worth through grades. Grades are important, but learning is more important.
>
> *Carol Dweck*

GROWTH MINDSETS AND FIXED MINDSETS

It turns out that psychologist Carol Dweck and others have studied the way I approached learning as an undergraduate. Apparently my approach is fairly common. Psychologists call it a "fixed mindset." The opposite is a "growth mindset." As I describe these mindsets, see if they sound familiar.

Learners with a **fixed mindset** believe people are born with a fixed amount of ability and talent. When it comes to intelligence, they've either got it or they don't. If they do well in school, it's because they're smart. If they don't do well in school, it's because they aren't. Dweck found that students with a fixed mindset prefer tasks they can already do well. New challenges are threatening because they fear their intelligence may not be up to the task. Thus, when they encounter a challenge, they tend to avoid it or quit as a method of self-protection. Mistakes and failures scare them because, in their mindset, such outcomes reflect poorly on their fixed level of intelligence. I've seen students complete all of the courses they need to graduate except one. That course is inevitably in the subject they fear: perhaps math, writing, or a foreign language. When students with a fixed mindset experience a challenge, setback, or failure, their inner chatter judges them (*I'm just not smart enough*) and they may give up. Does this sound like Victim behavior to you?

> . . . a miracle is just a shift in perception.
>
> *Marianne Williamson*

By contrast, learners with a **growth mindset** believe that intelligence is like a muscle—it gets stronger the more it's used. Interestingly, this mindset is consistent with what we know about how the brain learns. As mentioned in Chapter 1, the more we exercise our brains, the more neural networks are created and the "smarter" we become. A growth mindset encourages us to accept challenges, to work hard, to learn from mistakes, to change course if needed, and to keep going despite setbacks and failures. Learners in this mindset believe their hard work and persistence can overcome initial difficulties in mastering a subject or a skill. If what they are doing isn't working, their Inner Guide explains,

"I didn't work hard enough" or "There's a better way to do it," or both. They accept responsibility and they make a new plan. I trust that by now you recognize the response of a Creator.

Dweck has tested her theory about fixed and growth mindsets on students from preschool through college. One was an experiment with pre-med students at an Ivy League university. These students were taking a very challenging course in organic chemistry. The stakes were high because their grade in the course would play a big role in whether or not they got into medical school. Students with a growth mindset distinguished themselves from students with a fixed mindset in three important ways: (1) they enjoyed the course more, (2) they more effectively bounced back from setbacks such as poor test scores, and (3) their final grades were higher.

Psychologist Joshua Aronson and colleagues also tested Dweck's theory. They asked Stanford University students to be pen pals with local middle school students and help the younger students stay in school. The experimenters asked the Stanford students to tell their young pen pals things such as "Humans are capable of learning and mastering new things at any time in their lives." In other words, the Stanford students were encouraging their young pen pals to adopt a growth mindset. What the experimenters actually wanted to see was what impact expressing a growth mindset might have on the Stanford students. When later compared to a control group, the Stanford students in the experiment earned higher grades and reported more often that they enjoyed their academic work.

Dweck and others have explored what causes some people to adopt a fixed mindset while others take on the more empowering growth mindset. One explanation is that fixed mindsets result when important adults (e.g., parents or teachers) praise us for our intelligence: *You did so well in math. You're obviously very smart!* The message here is that success is the result of being smart. The problem is, now we're nervous about trying something new. After all, if we fail that means we're not smart enough . . . and we believe there's no way to get more "smarts." By contrast, a growth mindset is more likely to develop when important adults praise us for our effort (rather than our intelligence): *You did so well in math. You're obviously a hard worker!* The message here is that success is the result of effort. Armed with this belief, we're more likely to respond positively to future challenges because we're confident we can work harder if the outcome or experience is worth it.

Like other mindsets, fixed and growth mindsets seem to be shaped by deep-culture beliefs. For example, Japanese and Chinese parents are more likely to attribute success to a strong effort (growth mindset). They believe that all students can learn if they work hard enough. By contrast, North American parents are more likely to attribute success to inborn intelligence or ability (fixed mindset). This cultural belief shows up in the American educational system where "gifted" students are given enriched academic programs.

If you've developed a growth mindset, you have a core belief that will help you achieve success in college and beyond. However, if you realize you've developed a fixed mindset, you aren't stuck with it. You can revise your mindset.

The purpose of learning is growth, and our minds, unlike our bodies, can continue growing as we continue to live.

Mortimer Adler

If there is no dark and dogged will, there will be no shining accomplishment; if there is no dull and determined effort, there will be no brilliant achievement.

Chinese proverb

HOW TO DEVELOP A GROWTH MINDSET

Here are four ways to develop or strengthen a growth mindset.

Think of your brain as a muscle: Like a muscle, the more you use your brain, the "smarter" and more capable it becomes. The technical term is neuroplasticity. *Neuroplasticity* is the ability of your brain to use new experiences to revise old neural networks and create new ones. This is how learning happens. Once you understand this concept, you'll realize that—with mental effort—your brain is designed to grow and change. The idea that each human brain has a fixed capacity belongs on the scrapheap of faulty beliefs along with "the world is flat." Just because you may be challenged to learn something today doesn't mean that you can't learn it. Because of your brain's neuroplasticity, effort and persistence combined with effective study strategies are the keys to effective learning. For more information about this concept, revisit "Becoming an Active Learner" in Chapter 1.

Set learning goals . . . as well as performance goals: When I was an undergraduate, I set performance goals. My main goal was to see my grade point average improve every semester. I achieved that goal every semester, but I paid a price. To assure success, I played it safe, wasting many learning opportunities. I avoided courses that might have introduced me to a whole new world. I steered clear of "hard" professors who might have become mentors or guides. By studying only to get grades, I learned just enough to pass tests. Sure, I got a degree and, with it, a ticket into the world of employment . . . but at what cost? Don't misunderstand, there's nothing wrong with setting a goal to get good grades. Obviously, good grades are the means to many future goals, such as a job or graduate school. But there is something wrong if our *only* goal is to earn a grade. Such a goal limits our potential. It keeps us from developing knowledge, skills, and wisdom that could help us create a richer, more personally fulfilling life. The solution is to combine both kinds of goals. *Performance goals* provide you with measurable accomplishments (like grades), whereas *learning goals* offer knowledge and skills you can use for the rest of your life.

So, what would a learning goal look like? Suppose you're taking a writing class. A performance goal would be to earn an A in the course. A *learning* goal would be to master three ways to write an effective introductory paragraph. Suppose you want to lose weight. A performance goal would be to weigh 150 pounds by June 30. A learning goal would be to learn three important principles of good nutrition. Suppose you're taking an organic chemistry course. A *performance* goal would be to finish reading your text book by December 1. A *learning* goal would be to learn the discipline to read challenging content for at least 20 minutes without losing focus. Notice that performance goals usually give us a defined (often measurable) outcome. By contrast, learning

---

It's never too late to change your mindset. Mindsets are beliefs—powerful ones and ones that shape our motivation—but beliefs can be changed.

Carol Dweck

We now accept the fact that learning is a lifelong process of keeping abreast of change. And the most pressing task is to teach people how to learn.

Peter Drucker

goals help us grow, giving us skills and abilities we can use to achieve future performance goals. Whereas my *performance* goal might be to achieve x, my *learning goal* might be to learn five strategies to help me do x. Those same five strategies may also help me to achieve other goals for the rest of my life. Take a look back to the goals you set in Journal Entry 10 and see what kind of goals you created there. If they are mostly performance goals, consider adding a couple of learning goals.

Seek feedback: Feedback is essential to learning. Luckily, life offers us helpful feedback every day. Sadly, many ignore it . . . especially those with a fixed mindset. At first, feedback taps us politely on the shoulder. If we pay no attention, feedback shakes us vigorously. If we continue to ignore it, feedback may knock us to our knees, creating havoc in our lives. This havoc might be failing out of school or getting fired from a job. There's usually plenty of feedback long before the failure or firing if we will only heed its message. Your Inner Defender may see feedback as a threat, but your Inner Guide knows it is vital for success.

> Once you embrace unpleasant news, not as a negative but as evidence of a need for change, you aren't defeated by it. You're learning from it.
>
> *Bill Gates*

In college, think of yourself as an airplane pilot and your instructors as your personal air traffic controllers. When they correct you in class or write a comment on an assignment or give you a grade on a test, what they are really saying is, *You're on course, on course . . . whoops, now you're off course, off course . . . okay, that's right, now you're back on course.* Airplane pilots appreciate such feedback. Without it they might not get to their destination. They might even crash. Likewise, effective learners welcome their instructors' feedback and use it to stay on course. They heed every suggestion that instructors offer on assignments; they understand the message in their test scores; they request clarification of any feedback they don't understand; and they ask for additional feedback. Maybe the idea of paying attention to feedback sounds obvious to you, but I can't tell you how many students I've known who made the same mistakes over and over, ignoring both my feedback and the reality that when you keep doing what you've been doing, you'll keep getting what you've been getting.

Everywhere in life, heeding feedback is vital to creating the life you want. The feedback may be something said by friends, lovers, spouses, parents, children, neighbors, bosses, coworkers, and even strangers. Or it may be more subtle, coming in the form of an unsatisfying relationship, a boring job, blackouts from drinking too much, or runaway credit card debt. Any areas of discomfort or distress are red flags of warning: *Hey, wake up! You're headed away from your desired outcomes and experiences. You're off course!* And that awareness leads to a fourth way for developing a growth mindset.

> All human beings are periodically tested by the power of the universe . . . how one performs under pressure is the true measure of one's spirit, heart, and desire.
>
> *Spike Lee*

Change course when needed: It's one thing to realize you are off course. It's quite another to do something about it. Course correction takes courage. You need to admit that what you are doing isn't working, seek alternatives, abandon the familiar, and to walk into the unknown. Victims stay stuck. Creators learn, change, and grow.

> The capacity to correct course is the capacity to reduce the differences between the path you are on now and the optimal path to your objective....
>
> Charles Garfield

One of my off-course students was feeling overwhelmed by all she had to do, and then she made a course correction, changing the way she tackled large projects. In her journal she wrote, "When I break a huge task into chunks and do a little bit every day, I can accomplish great things."

Another off-course student discovered he was an expert at blaming his failures in college on other people: his boss, his teachers, his parents, his girlfriend. He decided to change and hold himself more responsible. He learned, "In the past I have spent more energy on getting people to feel sorry for me than I have on accomplishing something worthwhile."

A third off-course student was filled with hate for her father, who she felt had abandoned her, and then she decided to change. She forgave him and moved on with her life. She wrote, "Spending all of my time hating someone leaves me little time to love myself."

A fourth off-course student realized how little effort and care he put into everything he did, including his college assignments. He discovered, "I'm always looking for ways to cut corners, to get out of doing what's necessary. It doesn't work. I have to do my best in order to be successful."

And one more off-course student realized that the only goal he'd ever set in school was to get good grades. As a graduate student, he discovered, "When I focus on learning, my grades take care of themselves. Better yet, I learn things I can use to improve the quality of my life!" He regretted all of the learning he had missed out on, but he got excited by all there still is to learn. He started taking courses that excited him. He found new ways to apply what he was learning and created a whole new life for himself. He was grateful that he had given himself the gift of a major course correction, one that changed his outcomes and experiences. In case you haven't guessed, I was this off-course student.

We seldom move toward our goals and dreams in a straight line. With constant course corrections, however, we improve our chances of getting there eventually. And along the way, the University of Life offers us exactly the lessons we need to develop our full potential. We only have to listen, learn, change, and grow.

> To me, earth is a school. I view life as my classroom. My approach to the experiences I have every day is that I am a student, and that all my experiences have something they can teach me. I am always asking myself, "What learning is available for me now?"
>
> Mary Hulnick, vice-president, University of Santa Monica

 **Journal Entry 25**

In this activity, you will explore course corrections you have made or you need to make to improve your outcomes and experiences.

Make a choice: Write about one of the following:

A. Describe an important course correction you have made in the past. Explain how you became aware that you were off course, what you did to change course, and how your efforts turned out. Most important, what did you learn from this experience?

Discovering Your Preferred Ways of Learning

 **FOCUS QUESTIONS** What is your preferred way of learning? What can you do when your instructor doesn't teach the way you prefer to learn?

Today, we're well into the information age. That means staying on course to our goals and dreams requires learning vast amounts of information, facts, theories, and skills. Once you master the CORE Learning System introduced in Chapter 1, all that learning should be easy, right? Not quite.

You see, in addition to learning approaches that are common to us all, each of us has our own preferred learning experiences. Each of us has our own favored ways of taking in and deeply processing our learning experiences. Each of us has our own preferred ways of creating meaning from the rush and jumble of information we encounter in college, at work, at home, and everywhere else in life. Knowing how *you* prefer to learn gives you a great advantage everywhere in life, but especially in college when you get an instructor who doesn't teach the way you prefer to learn.

> It is very natural to teach in the same way we learn. It may be difficult for us to believe that others could learn in a way that is foreign and difficult for us.
>
> *Carolyn Mamchur*

SELF-ASSESSMENT: HOW I PREFER TO LEARN

Before reading on, take the following self-assessment inventory. It will give you insights about how you prefer to gather and process information.

LEARNING PREFERENCE INVENTORY

In each group below, rank all four answers (A, B, C, D) from the least true of you to the most true of you. Give each possible answer a different score. There are no right or wrong answers; your opinion is all that matters. Remember, items that are MOST TRUE OF YOU get a 4. You can also take this self-assessment online by accessing the CourseMate for *On Course* at www.cengagebrain.com.

Least true of you ← 1 2 3 4 → Most true of you

1. I would prefer to take a college course
   _____ A. in science.
   _____ B. in business management.
   _____ C. in group dynamics.
   _____ D. as an independent study that I design.

2. I solve problems by
   _____ A. standing back, thinking, and analyzing what is wrong.
   _____ B. doing something practical and seeing how it works.
   _____ C. leaping in and doing what feels right at the time.
   _____ D. trusting my intuition.
3. Career groups that appeal to me are
   _____ A. engineer, researcher, financial planner.
   _____ B. administrator, city manager, military officer.
   _____ C. teacher, social worker, physical therapist.
   _____ D. entrepreneur, artist, inventor.
4. Before I make a decision, I need to be sure that
   _____ A. I understand all of the relevant ideas and facts.
   _____ B. I'm confident my solution will work.
   _____ C. I know how my decision will affect others.
   _____ D. I haven't overlooked a more creative solution.
5. I believe that
   _____ A. life today needs more logical thinking and less emotion.
   _____ B. life rewards the practical, hard-working, down-to-earth person.
   _____ C. life must be lived with enthusiasm and passion.
   _____ D. life, like music, is best composed by creative inspiration, not by rules.
6. I would enjoy reading a book titled
   _____ A. *Great Theories and Ideas of the Twentieth Century.*
   _____ B. *How to Organize Your Life and Accomplish More.*
   _____ C. *The Keys to Developing Better Relationships.*
   _____ D. *Tapping into Your Creative Genius.*
7. I believe the most valuable information for making decisions comes from
   _____ A. logical analysis of facts.
   _____ B. what has worked in the past.
   _____ C. gut feelings.
   _____ D. my imagination.
8. I am persuaded by an argument that
   _____ A. offers statistical or factual proof.
   _____ B. presents the findings of recognized experts.
   _____ C. is passionately presented by someone I admire.
   _____ D. explores innovative possibilities for future change.
9. I prefer a teacher who
   _____ A. lectures knowledgeably about the important facts and theories of the subject.
   _____ B. provides practical, step-by-step, hands-on activities with clear learning objectives.
   _____ C. stimulates exciting class discussions and group projects.
   _____ D. challenges me to think for myself and explore the subject in my own way.

10. People who know me would describe me as
　　_____ A. logical.
　　_____ B. practical.
　　_____ C. emotional.
　　_____ D. creative.

Total your 10 scores for each letter and record them below:

_____ A. THINKING　　　_____ C. FEELING
_____ B. DOING　　　　_____ D. INNOVATING

Your scores suggest the following:

30–40　You have a strong preference to learn this way.
20–29　You are capable of learning this way when necessary.
10–19　You avoid this way of learning.

Each of us develops preferred ways of learning. These preferred ways of learning are more pleasurable, require less effort, and usually produce more successful learning than a less preferred learning experience. For a quick understanding of learning preferences, recall the last time you learned a new video game or assembled something with a number of parts. Some people prefer to start playing or assembling immediately. They dive right in. Other people prefer to read the directions first. Only after they digest the written information do they start playing or assembling. Notice that you could approach these learning tasks either way, but you *prefer* one learning experience over the other.

Although there is no preferred way for everyone to learn, there is a preferred way or ways for *you* to learn. Your scores on the self-assessment indicate your order of preference for four different learning approaches: THINKING, DOING, FEELING, and INNOVATING. More specifically, your scores suggest what types of questions motivate you, how you prefer to gather relevant information, and how you prefer to process information to discover meaningful answers.

Traditional college teaching is characterized by lectures and textbook assignments. These learning experiences typically favor the learning preference of Thinkers, and, to a somewhat lesser degree, Doers. However, as more instructors discover the importance of learning preferences, many are adapting their teaching methods to help all learners maximize their academic potential.

Knowledge of our brain dominance empowers us as individuals and groups to achieve more of our full potential.

Ned Herrmann

> Education is our passport to the future, for tomorrow belongs to the people who prepare for it today.... Give your brain as much attention as you do your hair and you'll be a thousand times better off.
>
> *Malcolm X*

As you might guess, you're bound to get instructors whose teaching methods don't match your learning preference(s). When you do, experiment with some of the suggestions that follow. Perhaps most important of all, develop flexibility in how you learn. The more choices you have, the richer your learning experience will be and the greater your success.

In the table on pages 228–229, you'll discover how Thinkers, Doers, Feelers, and Innovators prefer to learn. You may want to start by reading the section about your own learning preference(s), based on your self-assessment score. There you'll find options to use when your instructors don't teach as you prefer to learn. By looking at the other learning preferences as well, you'll see additional ways to expand your menu of effective learning strategies. Your goal here is to find deep-processing strategies that are compatible with and supportive of your preferred way(s) of learning as well as to expand your ability to learn in many ways.

Highly effective learners realize that not all instructors will create the kind of learning experiences they prefer. They take responsibility for not only *what* they learn but also *how* they learn it. They are confident that, with smart studying and persistence, their brains are up to the task. They discover deep-processing methods that maximize their learning, regardless of the subject or the way the instructor teaches.

	Thinking Learners	Doing Learners	Feeling Learners	Innovating Learners
Motivating questions that energize	**"What?" questions** *What theory supports that claim? What does a statistical analysis show? What is the logic here? What facts do you have? What experts have written about this?*	**"How?" questions** *How does this work? How can I use this? How will this help me or others? How did this work in the past? How can I do this more efficiently? How do experts do this?*	**"Why?" or "Who?" questions** *Why do I want or need to know this subject? Who is going to teach me? Who is going to learn this with me? Why do they want to know this information? Who here cares about me? Whom here do I care about?*	**"What if?" or "What else?" questions** *What if I tried doing this another way? What else could I do with this? What if the situation were different? What is this similar to?*
Preferred ways of gathering information	• enjoy pondering facts and theories • learn well from instructors who present information with lectures, visual aids, PowerPoint slides, instructor-modeled problem solving, textbook readings, independent library research, and activities that call upon logical skills, such as debates • benefit from time to reflect on what they are learning	• enjoy taking action • learn well from instructors who present factual information and practical skills in a step-by-step, logical manner; who present models or examples from experts in the field; and who allow students to do hands-on work in guided labs or practice applications • benefit from the opportunity to dive right in and do the work	• enjoy personal connections and an emotionally supportive environment • learn well from instructors who are warm and caring; who value feelings as well as thoughts; who create a safe, accepting classroom atmosphere with activities such as group work, role-playing, and sharing of individual experiences • benefit from an opportunity to relate personally with both their instructors and classmates	• enjoy imagining new possibilities and making unexpected connections • learn well from instructors who encourage students to discover new and innovative applications; who allow students to use their intuition to create something new; and who use approaches such as independent projects, flexible rules and deadlines, a menu of optional assignments, metaphors, art projects, and visual aids • benefit from the freedom to work independently and let their imaginations run free
Preferred ways of processing information	• respect logical argument supported by documented facts and data • are uncomfortable with answers that depend on tradition, emotion, personal considerations, or intuition • excel at analyzing, dissecting, figuring out, and using logic to arrive at reasoned answers • like well-organized and well-documented information • benefit from deep-processing strategies that bring order to complex information, such as creating outlines or comparison charts	• honor objective testing of an idea or theory, whether their own or an expert's • are uncomfortable with answers based on abstract theories, emotion, personal considerations, or intuition • excel at being unbiased, taking action and observing outcomes, following procedures, and using confirmed facts to arrive at reasoned answers • appreciate well-organized and well-documented information • benefit from deep-processing strategies that bring order to complex information, such as creating flow charts or a model of the concepts to be learned	• honor their emotions and seek answers that are personally meaningful • are uncomfortable with answers based on abstract theories or dispassionate facts and data • excel at responding to emotional currents in groups, empathizing with others, considering others' feelings in making decisions, and using empathy and gut feelings to arrive at personally relevant answers	• honor personal imagination and intuition • are uncomfortable with answers based on abstract theories, cold facts, hard data, emotion, or personal considerations • excel at trusting their inner vision, their intuitive sense of novel and exciting possibilities, and their imaginations

	Thinking Learners	Doing Learners	Feeling Learners	Innovating Learners
When your instructor doesn't teach to your preferred style *What you can do:*	• Construct important "What?" questions and search for their answers in class sessions and homework assignments. • Construct and answer other types of questions your instructor might ask: How? Who? Why? What if? • Read all of your textbook assignments carefully, creating well-organized notes that identify the key points. • Resist getting upset if your instructor asks you to work in groups or has students do some of the teaching. • Organize your lecture and reading notes in a logical fashion, using outlines and comparison charts wherever appropriate. • Study with classmates who have different preferred ways of learning from your own, as they may provide insights about how to learn best from your instructor's teaching style. • Demonstrate the step-by-step solution of a math or science problem. • Provide data or other objective evidence that supports theories presented.	• Construct important "How?" questions and search for their answers. • Construct and answer other types of questions your instructor might ask: What? Who? Why? What if? • Practice using the course information or skills outside of class. • Find someone who uses the course information or skills in his or her work and shadow that person for a day or more. • Resist getting upset if your instructor seems more interested in theories than in application. • Organize your lecture and reading notes in a step-by-step fashion, using outlines and comparison charts wherever appropriate. • Study with classmates who have preferred ways of learning different from your own, as they may provide insights into how to learn best from your instructor's teaching style.	• Construct important "Who?" and "Why?" questions and search for their answers. • Construct and answer other types of questions your instructor might ask: What? How? What if? • Discover the value of this subject for you personally. • Organize your notes and study materials using concept maps. • Resist feeling upset if your instructor seems distant or aloof. • Practice using the course information or skill with people in your life. • Make friends with classmates and discuss the subject with them outside of class. • Record class sessions (with permission) and listen to the recordings during free time. • Study with classmates who have different preferred ways of learning from your own, as they may provide insights into how to learn best from your instructor's teaching style. • Teach what you are learning to someone else.	• Construct important "What if?" and "What else?" questions and search for their answers. • Construct and answer other types of questions your instructor might ask: What? How? Who? Why? • Resist feeling upset when your instructor or classmates don't immediately see something as you do. • Organize your notes and study materials using concept maps and personally meaningful symbols or pictures. • Think about the content creatively (how could I adapt this?) and metaphorically (what is this like?). • Study with classmates who have different preferred ways of learning from your own, as they may provide insights into how to learn best from your instructor's teaching style.
Ask your instructor to do the following:	• Answer your important "What?" questions in class or in a conference. • List important points on the board or on handouts. • Provide handouts of PowerPoint presentations. • Allow students time to answer discussion questions in writing before answering them aloud. • Suggest additional readings, especially those written by recognized authorities in the subject. • Provide examples of past test questions. • Demonstrate the step-by-step solution of a math or science problem. • Provide data or other objective evidence that supports theories presented.	• Answer your important "How?" questions in class or in a conference. • Explain practical applications for theories taught in the course. • Provide a visual model of the concept (such as the Scripts Model in Chapter 6). • List important steps on the board or on handouts. • Demonstrate the information or skill in a step-by-step manner. • Invite guest speakers who can explain real-world application of the course information or skill in their daily work. • Observe and give corrective feedback as you demonstrate your hands-on understanding of the subject.	• Answer your important "Who?" and "Why?" questions in class or in a conference. • Explain how you might make a personal application of the course information. • Meet with your instructor outside of class, perhaps for tutoring, so you can get to know one another better and feel more comfortable in the class. • Provide occasional opportunities for small-group activities within the classroom. • Tell stories about how he or she (or someone else) has personally used the information or skills taught in the course. • Let you do some of the course assignments with a partner or in a group. • Allow students time to talk in pairs about discussion questions before answering them in front of the whole class.	• Answer your important "What if?" and "What else?" questions in class or in a conference. • Allow you to design some of your own assignments for the course. • Use visual aids to explain concepts in class. • Recommend a book for you to read by the most innovative or rebellious thinker in the field. • Evaluate your learning with essays and independent projects rather than with objective tests.

Employing Critical Thinking

 **Focus Questions** How can you determine the truth in this complex and confusing world? How can you present your truths in a way that is logical and persuasive to others?

Imagine this: While deciding what classes to take next semester, you decide to register for Psychology 101. After checking the various times it will be offered, you're delighted to discover that one section of the course fits perfectly into your schedule. The instructor is Professor Skinner. Because two of your friends are taking the course with Professor Skinner this semester, you wisely ask for their opinions.

One friend says, "Dr. Skinner is terrible. Don't even think about taking his course!" But your second friend says, "Dr. Skinner is the best instructor I've ever had! You should definitely take his class." Darn. Now what do you do?

Before deciding, you'd be smart to apply some critical thinking. The term "critical" derives from the Greek word *kritikos*, which means having the ability to understand or decide by using sound judgment. Critical thinking helps us better understand our complex world, make wise choices, and create more of our desired outcomes and experiences. Because they know the importance of critical thinking in many realms of life, most college educators place it high on the list of skills they want their students to master.

Here's good news. You've already been using a powerful critical thinking skill—the Wise Choice Process. As you've experienced, thoughtfully answering the six questions of the Wise Choice Process guides you through the steps of identifying options, looking at likely outcomes, and choosing the best option(s) available at the time. Making wise choices, then, is a key use of critical thinking.

In addition, critical thinking helps in another important realm: constructing and analyzing persuasive arguments. Think of the countless times others have tried to persuade you to think or do something: *Mathematics is a fascinating subject* (think this), *Let me copy your chemistry notes* (do that), *Global warming*

> Higher-order thinking, critical thinking abilities, are increasingly crucial to success in every domain of personal and professional life.
>
> *Richard Paul*

is a huge threat (think this), *Major in accounting* (do that), *My roommate is so inconsiderate* (think this), *Go to graduate school* (do that). And, of course, you're doing the same to them. Think this . . . do that.

Thus, much of life is a mental tug-of-war. Efforts to influence others' thoughts and actions lie at the heart of most human interaction, from conversations to wars. Think this . . . do that. It's no wonder the quality of your life is so greatly affected by your ability to construct and analyze persuasive arguments. You can even use these skills to decide whether or not to register for Professor Skinner's Psychology 101 class.

CONSTRUCTING LOGICAL ARGUMENTS

At many colleges, entire courses, even majors, are devoted to the study of argumentation. Here, we'll focus on two skills that are essential to the construction and analysis of persuasive arguments. The first skill is the ability to **construct a *logical argument***. Three components of a logical argument are (1) reasons, (2) evidence, and (3) conclusions. As the building blocks of a logical argument, these ingredients may be offered in any order. Suppose, for example, someone wants to convince you to participate in your college's Sophomore Year Abroad Program. Here's how she might present her argument: *You should apply for our college's Sophomore Year Abroad Program. It'll change your life. I read an article in our college newspaper about the Sophomore Year Abroad Program. The author surveyed students who have completed the program, and 80 percent rated their experience as "life changing."*

Here's what this argument looks like when organized by its components:

1. REASONS (also called *premises, claims,* or *assumptions*) answer the question "Why?" Reasons explain why the audience should think or do something. Reasons are presented as true, but they may not be.	**WHY?** *The Sophomore Year Abroad Program will change your life.*
2. EVIDENCE (also called *support*) answers the question "How do you know?" Evidence provides support to explain how the persuader knows the reason(s) to be true. Evidence should be verifiable as true. Three common kinds of evidence are facts, data, and stories.	**HOW DO I KNOW?** *I read an article in our college newspaper about the Sophomore Year Abroad Program. The author surveyed students who have completed the program, and 80 percent rated their experience as "life changing."*
3. CONCLUSIONS (also called *opinions, beliefs,* or *positions*) answer the question "What?" Conclusions state what the persuader wants the audience to think or do.	**WHAT SHOULD YOU THINK OR DO?** *You should apply for our college's Sophomore Year Abroad Program.*

ASKING PROBING QUESTIONS

Essential to analyzing a logical argument is a second critical thinking skill: **asking probing questions**. A probing question exposes conclusions built on unsound reasons, flawed evidence, and faulty logic. Probing questions are the kind that a good lawyer, doctor, educator, parent, detective, lover, shopper, or

---

Intelligence is something we are born with. Thinking is a skill that must be learned.

Edward de Bono

The problem with many youngsters today is not that they don't have opinions but that they don't have the facts on which to base their opinions.

Albert Shanker

friend asks to expose a hidden truth. The following chart lists some of the questions that critical thinkers might ask of any persuasive argument. Asking and answering these questions (and others) can help you both construct powerful arguments of your own and analyze the arguments of others.

Questions About Reasons	Sample Probing Questions
• What reasons have been offered to support the conclusion?	• When your brother studied for a year in Australia, was the experience life changing for him?
• Based on your experience and knowledge, do the reasons make sense?	• What did the students mentioned in the newspaper article mean by "life changing"?
• Did the reasons derive from careful reflection and logical thinking, or are they misguided beliefs or prejudices?	• Does it seem likely that such a program would change my life?
• Are there important exceptions to the reason?	• Do I even want to change my life?
• Are the definitions of all key terms clear?	
• Are strong emotions being substituted for reasons?	
Questions About Evidence	**Sample Probing Questions**
• Is the source of the evidence reliable?	• Could the group of students polled have been specially selected to support the author's point of view about the Sophomore Year Abroad Program?
• Is the evidence true?	
• Is the evidence objective and unbiased?	
• Is the evidence relevant?	
• Is the evidence current?	• Does the person persuading me stand to gain if I choose to participate in the program?
• Is there enough evidence?	
• Does contradictory evidence exist?	• Were enough students polled to make their results significant?
• Is the evidence complete?	
	• What percent of students from all previous Sophomore Year Abroad groups rated the experience as "life changing"?
Questions About Conclusions	**Sample Probing Questions**
• Why?	• Could there be another cause for the students' life-changing experiences besides the Sophomore Year Abroad Program?
• Is the conclusion logical, or are there errors in the reasoning?	
• Could a different conclusion be drawn from the same reasons and/or evidence?	• Did the students who rated their experience as "life changing" have anything else in common that might have been the cause of their life-changing outcome instead of the program?
	• Is the program today the same program that changed the lives of students in the survey?

> Always the beautiful answer who asks a more beautiful question.
>
> *e.e. cummings*

> The real value of learning lies in answering questions and questioning answers.
>
> *Marty Grothe*

APPLYING CRITICAL THINKING

Let's observe these critical thinking skills in action. Listen in as two students debate their conclusions about the biology professor described in "A Fish Story" (the case study that opens this chapter). Note how they explain the reasons and

Planning Your Next Steps

 **Focus Questions** How have you changed while writing your journal entries? What changes do you still want to make?

Although our travels together are coming to an end, your journey has really just begun. Look out there to your future. What do you want to have, do, or be? What actions do you need to take to achieve your desired outcomes and experiences? Make a plan and go for it!

Sure, you'll get off course at times. But now you have the strategies—both outer and inner—to get back on course. Before heading out toward your goals and dreams, take a moment to review those strategies. Anytime you want, you can look over the table of contents of this book for an overview of what you've learned. Scan the chapter-opening charts to review the choices of successful and struggling people. Reread a strategy as a reminder. Review the study skills you chose to create your CORE Learning System. Perhaps most important of all, reread your journal. At any time you can return to *On Course* and to your journal to remind yourself of anything you forget. And, believe me, you *will* forget. But you have the power to remember . . . and to make wise choices . . . and to achieve the life of your dreams.

ASSESS YOURSELF, AGAIN

On the next page is a duplicate of the self-assessment you took in Chapter 1. Take it again. (Don't look back at your previous answers yet.) In Journal Entry 33, you will compare your first scores with your scores today, and you'll consider the changes you have made. Acknowledge yourself for your courage to grow. Look, also, at the changes you still need to make to become your best self.

You now have much of what you need to stay on course to the life of your dreams. The rest you can learn on your journey. Be bold! Begin today!

Onward!

> Destiny is not a matter of chance; it is a matter of choice. It is not a thing to be waited for; it is a thing to be achieved.
>
> *William Jennings Bryant*

> It isn't where you came from; it's where you're going that counts.
>
> *Ella Fitzgerald*

SELF-ASSESSMENT

Visit www.cengagebrain.com to access this *On Course* self-assessment online through CourseMate for *On Course*.

You're about to retake the self-assessment you took in Chapter 1. For now, it's important that you **do not look back at your scores from Chapter 1**. You'll be able to do that in just a little while.

First, read the following 64 statements. Decide how true you believe each statement was about you at the *beginning* of this course. Write that score in the column labeled "THEN."

Next, decide how true you believe that same statement is about you at the *end* of this course. Write the score in the column labeled "NOW."

To get an accurate picture of yourself, consider what you remember **WAS** honestly true about you at the beginning of the course and what you believe **IS** honestly true about you now. Remember, there are no right or wrong answers. Assign each statement two scores (THEN and NOW) from 0 to 10, as follows:

Totally False ← 0 1 2 3 4 5 6 7 8 9 10 → Totally True

	THEN	NOW	
1.	_____	_____	I control how successful I will be.
2.	_____	_____	I'm not sure why I'm in college.
3.	_____	_____	I spend most of my time doing important things.
4.	_____	_____	When I encounter a challenging problem, I try to solve it by myself.
5.	_____	_____	When I get off course from my goals and dreams, I realize it right away.
6.	_____	_____	I'm not sure how I prefer to learn.
7.	_____	_____	Whether I'm happy or not depends mostly on me.
8.	_____	_____	I'll truly accept myself only after I eliminate my faults and weaknesses.
9.	_____	_____	Forces out of my control (such as poor teaching) are the cause of low grades I receive in school.
10.	_____	_____	I place great value on getting my college degree.
11.	_____	_____	I don't need to write things down because I can remember what I need to do.
12.	_____	_____	I have a network of people in my life that I can count on for help.
13.	_____	_____	If I have habits that hinder my success, I'm not sure what they are.
14.	_____	_____	When I don't like the way an instructor teaches, I know how to learn the subject anyway.
15.	_____	_____	When I get very angry, sad, or afraid, I do or say things that create a problem for me.
16.	_____	_____	When I think about performing an upcoming challenge (such as taking a test), I usually see myself doing well.
17.	_____	_____	When I have a problem, I take positive actions to find a solution.
18.	_____	_____	I don't know how to set effective short-term and long-term goals.
19.	_____	_____	I am organized.

20. _____ _____ When I take a difficult course in school, I study alone.
21. _____ _____ I'm aware of beliefs I have that hinder my success.
22. _____ _____ I'm not sure how to think critically and analytically about complex topics.
23. _____ _____ When choosing between doing an important school assignment or something really fun, I do the school assignment.
24. _____ _____ I break promises that I make to myself or to others.
25. _____ _____ I make poor choices that keep me from getting what I really want in life.
26. _____ _____ I expect to do well in my college classes.
27. _____ _____ I lack self-discipline.
28. _____ _____ I listen carefully when other people are talking.
29. _____ _____ I'm stuck with any habits of mine that hinder my success.
30. _____ _____ My intelligence is something about myself that I can improve.
31. _____ _____ I often feel bored, anxious, or depressed.
32. _____ _____ I feel just as worthwhile as any other person.
33. _____ _____ Forces outside of me (such as luck or other people) control how successful I will be.
34. _____ _____ College is an important step on the way to accomplishing my goals and dreams.
35. _____ _____ I spend most of my time doing unimportant things.
36. _____ _____ I am aware of how to show respect to people who are different from me (race, religion, sexual orientation, age, etc.).
37. _____ _____ I can be off course from my goals and dreams for quite a while without realizing it.
38. _____ _____ I know how I prefer to learn.
39. _____ _____ My happiness depends mostly on what's happened to me lately.
40. _____ _____ I accept myself just as I am, even with my faults and weaknesses.
41. _____ _____ I am the cause of low grades I receive in school.
42. _____ _____ If I lose my motivation in college, I don't know how I'll get it back.
43. _____ _____ I have a written self-management system that helps me get important things done on time.
44. _____ _____ I seldom interact with people who are different from me.
45. _____ _____ I'm aware of the habits I have that hinder my success.
46. _____ _____ If I don't like the way an instructor teaches, I'll probably do poorly in the course.
47. _____ _____ When I'm very angry, sad, or afraid, I know how to manage my emotions so I don't do anything I'll regret later.
48. _____ _____ When I think about performing an upcoming challenge (such as taking a test), I usually see myself doing poorly.
49. _____ _____ When I have a problem, I complain, blame others, or make excuses.
50. _____ _____ I know how to set effective short-term and long-term goals.
51. _____ _____ I am disorganized.
52. _____ _____ When I take a difficult course in school, I find a study partner or join a study group.

53. _____ _____ I'm unaware of beliefs I have that hinder my success.
54. _____ _____ I know how to think critically and analytically about complex topics.
55. _____ _____ I often feel happy and fully alive.
56. _____ _____ I keep promises that I make to myself or to others.
57. _____ _____ When I have an important choice to make, I use a decision-making process that analyzes possible options and their likely outcomes.
58. _____ _____ I don't expect to do well in my college classes.
59. _____ _____ I am a self-disciplined person.
60. _____ _____ I get distracted easily when other people are talking.
61. _____ _____ I know how to change habits of mine that hinder my success.
62. _____ _____ Everyone is born with a certain amount of intelligence, and there's not really much you can do to change that.
63. _____ _____ When choosing between doing an important school assignment or something really fun, I usually do something fun.
64. _____ _____ I feel less worthy than other people.

Transfer your scores to the scoring sheets on the next two pages. For each of the eight areas, total your scores in columns A and B. Then total your final scores as shown in the sample.

SELF-ASSESSMENT SCORING SHEET FOR "THEN" (BEGINNING OF COURSE)

SAMPLE

A	B
6. 8	29. 3
14. 5	35. 3
21. 6	50. 6
73. 9	56. 2

__28__ + 40 − __14__ = __54__

SCORE #1: ACCEPTING PERSONAL RESPONSIBILITY

A	B
1. ___	9. ___
17. ___	25. ___
41. ___	33. ___
57. ___	49. ___

___ + 40 − ___ = ___

SCORE #2: DISCOVERING SELF-MOTIVATION

A	B
10. ___	2. ___
26. ___	18. ___
34. ___	42. ___
50. ___	58. ___

___ + 40 − ___ = ___

SCORE #3: MASTERING SELF-MANAGEMENT

A	B
3. ___	11. ___
19. ___	27. ___
43. ___	35. ___
59. ___	51. ___

___ + 40 − ___ = ___

SCORE #4: EMPLOYING INTERDEPENDENCE

A	B
12. ___	4. ___
28. ___	20. ___
36. ___	44. ___
52. ___	60. ___

___ + 40 − ___ = ___

SCORE #5: GAINING SELF-AWARENESS

A	B
5. ___	13. ___
21. ___	29. ___
45. ___	37. ___
61. ___	53. ___

___ + 40 − ___ = ___

SCORE #6: ADOPTING LIFELONG LEARNING

A	B
14. ___	6. ___
30. ___	22. ___
38. ___	46. ___
54. ___	62. ___

___ + 40 − ___ = ___

SCORE #7: DEVELOPING EMOTIONAL INTELLIGENCE

A	B
7. ___	15. ___
23. ___	31. ___
47. ___	39. ___
55. ___	63. ___

___ + 40 − ___ = ___

SCORE #8: BELIEVING IN MYSELF

A	B
16. ___	8. ___
32. ___	24. ___
40. ___	48. ___
56. ___	64. ___

___ + 40 − ___ = ___

INTERPRETING YOUR SCORES

A score of . . .

- **0–39** Indicates an area where your choices will **seldom** keep you on course.
- **40–63** Indicates an area where your choices will **sometimes** keep you on course.
- **64–80** Indicates an area where your choices will **usually** keep you on course.

SELF-ASSESSMENT SCORING SHEET FOR "NOW" (END OF COURSE)

SAMPLE

A	B
6. _8_	29. _3_
14. _5_	35. _3_
21. _6_	50. _6_
73. _9_	56. _2_

_28_ + 40 − _14_ = _54_

SCORE #1: ACCEPTING PERSONAL RESPONSIBILITY

A	B
1. ___	9. ___
17. ___	25. ___
41. ___	33. ___
57. ___	49. ___

___ + 40 − ___ = ___

SCORE #2: DISCOVERING SELF-MOTIVATION

A	B
10. ___	2. ___
26. ___	18. ___
34. ___	42. ___
50. ___	58. ___

___ + 40 − ___ = ___

SCORE #3: MASTERING SELF-MANAGEMENT

A	B
3. ___	11. ___
19. ___	27. ___
43. ___	35. ___
59. ___	51. ___

___ + 40 − ___ = ___

SCORE #4: EMPLOYING INTERDEPENDENCE

A	B
12. ___	4. ___
28. ___	20. ___
36. ___	44. ___
52. ___	60. ___

___ + 40 − ___ = ___

SCORE #5: GAINING SELF-AWARENESS

A	B
5. ___	13. ___
21. ___	29. ___
45. ___	37. ___
61. ___	53. ___

___ + 40 − ___ = ___

SCORE #6: ADOPTING LIFELONG LEARNING

A	B
14. ___	6. ___
30. ___	22. ___
38. ___	46. ___
54. ___	62. ___

___ + 40 − ___ = ___

SCORE #7: DEVELOPING EMOTIONAL INTELLIGENCE

A	B
7. ___	15. ___
23. ___	31. ___
47. ___	39. ___
55. ___	63. ___

___ + 40 − ___ = ___

SCORE #8: BELIEVING IN MYSELF

A	B
16. ___	8. ___
32. ___	24. ___
40. ___	48. ___
56. ___	64. ___

___ + 40 − ___ = ___

INTERPRETING YOUR SCORES

A score of . . .

- **0–39** Indicates an area where your choices will **seldom** keep you on course.
- **40–63** Indicates an area where your choices will **sometimes** keep you on course.
- **64–80** Indicates an area where your choices will **usually** keep you on course.

CHOICES OF SUCCESSFUL STUDENTS

SUCCESSFUL STUDENTS...	STRUGGLING STUDENTS...
accept personal responsibility, seeing themselves as the primary cause of their outcomes and experiences	see themselves as victims, believing that what happens to them is determined primarily by external forces such as fate, luck, and powerful others.
discover self-motivation, finding purpose in their lives by discovering personally meaningful goals and dreams.	have difficulty sustaining motivation, often feeling depressed, frustrated, and/or resentful about a lack of direction in their lives.
master self-management, consistently planning and taking purposeful actions in pursuit of their goals and dreams.	seldom identify specific actions needed to accomplish a desired outcome, and when they do, they tend to procrastinate.
employ interdependence, building mutually supportive relationships that help them achieve their goals and dreams (while helping others do the same).	are solitary, seldom requesting, even rejecting, offers of assistance from those who could help.
gain self-awareness, consciously employing behaviors, beliefs, and attitudes that keep them on course.	make important choices unconsciously, being directed by self-sabotaging habits and outdated life scripts.
adopt lifelong learning, finding valuable lessons and wisdom in nearly every experience they have.	resist learning new ideas and skills, viewing learning as fearful or boring rather than as mental play.
develop emotional intelligence, effectively managing their emotions in support of their goals and dreams.	live at the mercy of strong emotions, such as anger, depression, anxiety, or a need for instant gratification.
believe in themselves, seeing themselves as capable, lovable, and unconditionally worthy human beings.	doubt their competence and personal value, feeling inadequate to create their desired outcomes and experiences.